Little Visits™
1-2-3

Little Visits™
1-2-3

Devotions for families with infant to pre-school children

By Mary Manz Simon
Illustrated by Rip Kastaris

Publishing House
St. Louis

Cover Illustrations by Joe Isom

Library of Congress Cataloging-in-Publication Data
Simon, Mary Manz.
    Little visits 1-2-3: devotions for families with very young children by Mary Manz Simon.
       —(Good news for families)
    ISBN 0-570-03082-X—ISBN 0-570-03081-1 (pbk.)
    1. Family—Prayer-books and devotions—English. 2. Children-visits one-two-
      three. I. Title. II. Title: Little visits one-two-three. III. Series.
BV255.S575 1990   89-38013
249—dc20   CIP

1 2 3 4 5 6 7 8 9 10   99 98 97 96 95 94 93 92 91 90

For Hank,
My partner in life

Contents

Preface

The place to begin using this book is on the floor. That is, after all, from where your child views God's world.

The young child's world isn't exotic. It's filled with everyday items, like sandboxes and favorite drinking cups. Places include "my" bedroom, "my" basement, "my" car . . . with an emphasis on "my." A young child feels the world revolves around him.

You are also a part of that world. You are among those who reflect God's love to a young child. You will be among the first to share the Good News of Jesus Christ as Savior and Lord.

In *Little Visits 1–2–3* you'll find devotional activities about shadows and storms, naptime and Christmas. Every page includes a special note for you, too. Included is information on child development, snack ideas, and even bits of encouragement. Suggested activities require thirty seconds or less preparation time. I guarantee that! After all, at one time my children were stairsteps aged 1, 2, and 3.

This is the third *Little Visits* book I've written. *Little Visits with Jesus*, a best-seller, was followed by *More Little Visits with Jesus*. And you now hold the book that comes before the others, the book that will be the first in your child's devotional library.

As an early childhood educator, I can already hear the question, "How soon can I begin using *Little Visits 1–2–3*?" Right now is the perfect time. If your child is six-months old or three-years old, share devotional time. Use this book informally. Take clues from your child about how long you spend together.

The actual time doing these activities and readings will seem short. But the memories will last a lifetime.

I pray God will bless you, your young child, and your "Little Visits" with Him.

Mary Manz Simon

From the very beginning the Word was
with God.

John 1:2

Let's Start

Let's get started; there are many ways.
Let's begin on this first page.
You make the sound or act the part
as we look at different ways to start.

Giddyup, giddyup!
The horsy starts.
Giddyup, giddyup!

On your mark, get set, go!
The runners are off.
On your mark, get set, go!

Shake hands, shake hands.
"How do you do?"
Shake hands, shake hands.

"Once upon a time," the book begins,
a child grows up with Jesus.
Keep on turning the pages . . . .

———————————

Dear Jesus,
    Help me to grow up with You.
    Be with me as I learn and do. Amen.

To the adult: *My prayer is that* Little Visits 1-2-3 *will enrich your life and the life of your young child this year. My hope is that this book will become very special for both of you. Personalize pages as you wish. Perhaps you'll mark in pencil the delightful responses from your child. Perhaps you'll want to jot down the dates on which you use individual devotions. I pray this book will help you and your child make wonderful memories.*

He gives food to every living creature.
Psalm 136:25

Food Roll

Instructions: Take a can of food and sit on the floor. As you go through the devotion, roll the can gently back and forth to your child.

God gives me food.
Roll the can.
I like good food.
Roll the can.
Food helps me grow.
Roll the can.
I'm growing up!
Roll the can.

Dear Jesus,
Thank You for food. Amen.

To the adult: *Help your child match "real" food with pictures on canned goods. For example, get a carrot out of the refrigerator and match with a carrot pictured on a label.*

He scatters snow like a blanket.
Psalm 147:16

Snow Fun

Instructions: Help your child act out this verse.

The snowflakes flutter to the ground.
I cannot hear a single sound.
I now will run outside to play.
Thank You, God, for snow today!

I wrap a scarf around me tight
And put my mittens on just right.
I run outside for fun and play.
Thank You, God, for snow today!

I roll and roll a great big ball.
Now see my snowman? Oh, so tall!
I like this kind of outside play.
Thank You, God, for snow today!

Dear Jesus,
I like to play outside in the snow. Amen.

To the adult: *Open your freezer. Ask your child to point to and name things that are as cold as snow.*

*I urge that . . . [prayers] be offered to
God.*   1 Timothy 2:1

I Pray

Instructions: Encourage your child to act out this verse.

I can pray like this
   with my hands together.
I can pray like this
   when I kneel at night.
I can pray like this
   with my arms across.
I can pray just any way
   and God says, "It's all right."

_____

Dear Jesus,
   I pray to You when _____ . Amen.

To the adults: *Help your child explore different respectful positions to use during prayer. Praying with arms folded across the chest—as people did in the medieval times—is just one way to pray. The "arms crossed" (or pretzel position, as children might say) simply crosses arms, not fingers, as we do when folding our hands to pray. These other postures might be interesting for your child to try.*

See how much the Father has loved us!
1 John 3:1

Emotions

Instructions: Encourage your child to act out this verse.

Sometimes I fuss
And stomp around,
But Jesus still loves me.

Sometimes I'm frightened,
So afraid,
But Jesus still loves me.

Sometimes I'm happy,
Smiling wide,
And Jesus still loves me.

Sometimes I'm angry,
Upset, and mad,
But Jesus still loves me.

What makes me feel so
Glad all over?
Jesus really loves me!

———————

Dear Jesus,
Thank You for loving me. Amen.

To the adult: *Parents spend several years helping their children identify their feelings. A simple verse like this can be a first step toward dealing with emotions in constructive, acceptable ways. During these early stages of emotional development, parents often pray for patience for their child and for themselves.*

Praise the Lord, because He is good.
Psalm 135:3

Happy Birthday!

Instructions: Help your child act out the riddles.

When it's my birthday, I
♦ blow out the _____ ,
♦ eat some _____ ,
♦ open a _____ ,
♦ listen while people sing _____ ,
♦ and give thanks.

_____

Dear Jesus,
A birthday, a birthday,
My birthday's just here.
I don't look much older
But thanks, God, for this year. Amen.

To the adult: *Help your child mark this year's calendar with his birthday. Encourage him to color around the space marking his day, put on a sticker, or do something else that will make the day special.*

*He sets . . . the time for saving and the
time for throwing away.*
Ecclesiastes 3:6

Cleanup Time

Instructions: Help your child act out this verse.

It's cleanup time.
I'll make the bed.
Thank You, God, for making me strong.

It's cleanup time.
I'll pick up the toys.
Thank You, God, for making me strong.

It's cleanup time.
I'll chase the dust.
Thank You, God, for making me strong.

It's cleanup time.
I'll wash my cup and plate.
Thank You, God, for making me strong.

———————

Dear Jesus,
Help me be a good helper. Amen.

To the adult: *This verse can be repeated during the day to help your child
have fun with chores and focus on God during the day.*

You created every part of me.
Psalm 139:13

Pairs

Instructions: Encourage your child to act out this verse.

God gave me a pair of hands.
I can clap them.

God gave me a pair of eyes.
I can blink them.

God gave me a pair of thumbs.
I can tap them.

God gave me a pair of feet.
I can touch them.

God gave me a pair of ears.
I can wiggle them.

———————

Dear Jesus,
Thanks for making me, me. Amen.

To the adult: *The concept of pairs might be new to your child. During the day, informally help your child identify pairs—shoes, forks, crayons, etc.*

Worship the Lord your God.
Luke 4:8

Where Are People Going?

Instructions: Help your child act out this verse.

People are driving here in cars.
Zoom, zoom, zoom go the motors.
People are riding here in buses.
Clink, clink, clink say the coins.
People are walking here on the sidewalk.
Walk, walk, walk go the feet.
Where are these people going?

People are driving here in cars: *zoom, zoom.*
People are riding here in buses: *clink, clink.*
People are walking here on foot: *walk, walk.*
It's time for church.

———————————

Dear Jesus,
I go to church by ——————————— . Amen.

To the adult: *Young children learn best by doing. Whenever possible, let your child experience different kinds of transportation. Your child might enjoy cutting out pictures of "things I've ridden in" or "things I'd like to ride" from today's newspaper.*

Let the earth produce all kinds of
animal life.   Genesis 1:24

Walking

Instructions: Encourage your child to act out this verse.

God made worms to "walk" like this:
    stretch-squoosh
    stretch-squoosh
That's how a worm "walks."

God made penguins to walk like this:
    waddle, waddle
    waddle, waddle
That's how a penguin walks.

God made elephants to walk like this:
    slowly step
    slowly step
That's how an elephant walks.

God made people to walk like this:
    walk, walk
    walk, walk
That's how I walk.

Dear Jesus,
    Thanks for my legs. Amen.

To the adult: *Do this verse again, but this time, let your child act it out letting her "fingers do the walking" in peanut butter play dough: simply mix 1 cup peanut butter, ⅔ cup honey, and ½ cup instant nonfat dry milk. (Tips: Refrigerate leftover play dough for use tomorrow. Tape down waxed paper on the table for easy clean-up.)*

I will always thank the Lord.
Psalm 34:1

Mmmmmm . . .

Instructions: Encourage your child to make the appropriate sounds.

I open my mouth and what do you hear?
Listen to me. Now stand very near.
♦ I can breathe.
♦ I can hiss.
♦ I can hum.
♦ I can sigh.
♦ I can cough.
♦ I can whisper, "Jesus loves me."

_____

Dear Jesus,
I love You, too. Amen.

To the adult: *Living with a young child often means living with sounds. One of the most effective ways to gain a moment of quiet is to borrow a technique from classroom teachers of young children. Simply whisper, "Listen to the silence."*

He spreads snow like a blanket.
Psalm 147:16

Snow Song

Instructions: Sing this to the tune "Three Blind Mice."

> God sends snow.
> God sends snow.
> Big snow flakes.
> Small snow flakes.
> Snow falls on houses and down the trees.
> It's carried all over by winter breeze.
> It sticks to my mittens and makes my nose
>   freeze.
> God sends snow.

> Dear Jesus,
>   When cold winds blow
>   And there is snow,
>   I'm glad I'm warm inside. Amen.

To the adult: *Water play can brighten up even the darkest winter day. When children are cooped up inside during these days, nothing soothes like water. The best water toys come from the kitchen: a funnel, turkey baster, and measuring spoons. After play in the sink or tub, your child will appreciate some nice-smelling lotion to keep his skin soft and smooth in the dry winter air.*

I lie down and sleep.

Psalm 3:5

Naptime

I've jumped and run.
I've had some fun.
I've played a bunch.
I've eaten lunch.
It's time to rest.
I'm in my nest.
It's naptime.

———————————

Dear Jesus,
    Thanks for the chance to come to bed
    And, on my pillow, rest my head. Amen.

To the adult: *One of the nicest aspects of a child going to sleep are the moments spent getting ready for bed. If we think back to our childhood, we might remember a favorite storybook, poem, or prayer. The routine you establish for naptime should settle a child down, establish a quiet mood, and, perhaps years from now, contribute to a happy memory.*

Fruit is sweet to my taste.
Song of Songs 2:3

Snacktime Song

Instructions: Encourage your child to show how she'd fix the various fruits as you sing to the tune, "Here We Go 'Round the Mulberry Bush."

Watch me as I peel a banana,
Peel a banana, peel a banana.
Watch me as I peel a banana.
Thank You, God, for fruit.

Watch me as I open the orange,
Open the orange, open the orange.
Watch me as I open the orange.
Thank You God, for fruit.

Watch me as I bite the apple,
Bite the apple, bite the apple.
Watch me as I bite the apple.
Thank You, God, for fruit.

———————————

Dear Jesus,
My favorite fruit is ——————— . Amen.

To the adult: *Enjoy a fruit break with your child.*

I am with you.

Isaiah 43:5

Feelings

Instructions: Encourage your child to act out this verse.

When I feel grumpy
This is how I frown.

When I'm excited
I jump up and down.

When I feel loving
My kisses are free.

When I am frightened
I need You by me.

———————————

Dear Jesus,
Thank You for being with me. Amen.

To the adult: *A child who is relaxed will talk openly about feelings. A good mid-winter relaxer is playing in the sink with shaving cream. Just squirt some out—your child can trace, draw, or just feel. It's also an easy way to clean the bathroom sink!*

Every kind of animal and bird . . .
went into the boat with Noah.

Genesis 7:8

Drip Drop

Instructions: Your child can say "drip, drop" at the end of each line until the end. Then help your child spread his arms to make a rainbow surprise.

Noah took a hammer. (*Drip, drop.*)
He pounded boards together. (*Drip, drop.*)
Noah built a big boat. (*Drip, drop.*)
The animals all lined up. (*Drip, drop.*)
Noah said, "All aboard." (*Drip, drop.*)
It rained and rained and rained. (*Drip, drop.*)
Noah looked. The rain had stopped. Surprise!

Dear Jesus,
When it rains I _____ . Amen.

To the adult: *Your child might enjoy recreating his own version of Noah's Ark. Stuffed animals can be lined up in pairs by a "boat."* (A laundry basket or cardboard box can be the boat.)

You belong to God, my children.
1 John 4:4

Go-togethers

Instructions: Encourage your child to make the various shapes using her fingers.

I can make a ball of snow.
Snow balls go together with winter.

I can make a heart.
Hearts go together with Valentine's Day.

I can make a tent.
Tents go together with vacation.

I can make a donut.
Donuts go together with my hungry tummy.

I can make a cross.
Jesus goes together with me.

Dear Jesus,
 Thank You for my fingers that do so
 many things. Amen.

To the adult: *Syrup shapes can brighten up mid-winter breakfast time. Cut out a simple shape in your child's pancake, then fill the hole with syrup. Or, simply pour on the syrup in a familiar shape. Does your child recognize what's on the pancake?*

God made them all.
Genesis 1:25

And the Sound Is . . .

Instructions: Encourage your child to make the appropriate noises.

A cow says _____ .
God made cows.

A chicken says _____ .
God made chickens.

A duck says _____ .
God made ducks.

A pig says _____ .
God made pigs.

A turkey says _____ .
God made turkeys.

God made me, too. But I'm special. I can say,
"Jesus loves me."

———————————

Dear Jesus,
I love You, too. Amen.

To the adult: *Have your child count the number of stuffed toys or plastic animals he has that, if real, might live on a farm.*

The greatest of these is love.
1 Corinthians 13:13

Hearts

Instructions: Encourage your child to act out this verse.

Snip, snip, cut a heart.
Cut a heart right from the start.

Slowly, slowly, move around.
Cut a heart without a sound.

Look, look, what do I see?
It's a heart made just by me!

Dear Jesus,
I will give a valentine to _____ . Amen.

To the adult: *Valentine's Day is a great holiday for even a young child. If your child can't cut yet, cut out a heart for her. Let her decorate it with glue and bits of red fabric and trim, or scraps of red wrapping paper. (Avoid paper doilies—they tear easily.) It will be easier for your child to give away a valentine she's made if she also keeps one of her masterpieces for herself!*

His love is eternal.
Psalm 136:1

Shakes

Instructions: Encourage your child to act out this verse.

What shakes?
◆ Salt shakes.
◆ Jelly shakes.
◆ Earthquakes shake.
◆ I shake.

God's love doesn't shake.
◆ It is quiet.
◆ It tiptoes around.
◆ It feels like a hug.

Dear Jesus,
    Thank You for Your love. Amen.

To the adult: *The concept of "Jesus as God's valentine" is really difficult for young children to understand. Children see that love reflected through people around them, like you. The sharing you do through the activities in this book is one way of demonstrating to a child, "Jesus loves you and so do I." Happy Valentine's Day to you and your young child.*

All night long the Lord protects me.
Psalm 3:5

Shadow Play

Sometimes at night when I get in bed
I'm ready to rest my tired head.
But I worry about the sounds I hear;
I think up noises that might come near.

That's when I lie in bed and take
My fingers and a cross I make.
The cross reminds me "Jesus is near."
All night long I know He's here.

Dear Jesus,
Thank You for watching over me
at night. Amen.

To the adult: *Shadow play can be more than child's play. Go outside on a bright winter day or set up a bright light to shine against an indoor wall. Then show your child how he can make shadow shapes. Your child might even like to take a flashlight and look at all the shadows made by different objects in the house. Seeing how shadows are made—and actually making shadows himself—can help a child understand light and darkness.*

There will always be cold and heat,
summer and winter, day and night.
Genesis 8:22

When Does It Snow?

Instructions: Encourage your child to act out these next lines.

When does it snow?
◆ not when the angels have a pillow fight!
◆ not when the wind blows white feathers!
◆ not when marshmallows fall from the sky!

Snow falls when the air above earth is so cold
the water drops freeze.
◆ Then I put on my snow pants.
◆ I put on my hat.
◆ I put on my mittens.
◆ I put on my boots,
◆ and go out to play.

Dear Jesus,
Thanks for snow. Amen.

To the adult: *A stick can be a wonderful snow toy. Your child can trace shapes,*
the first letter of her name, and even a valentine heart.

We feast on the abundant food You
provide.   Psalm 36:8

Knife, Fork, Spoon, and Fingers

Instructions: Get a knife, fork, and spoon for your child to use while acting out these words. Encourage your child to add words for filling in the blanks.

Spoons are nice
♦ for ice cream.
♦ for cereal.
♦ for _____ .

Forks are good
♦ for macaroni and cheese.
♦ for baked potatoes.
♦ for _____ .

Knives are good
♦ to spread jelly.
♦ to cut meat.
♦ to _____ .

Fingers are good
♦ for hot dogs.
♦ for apples.
♦ for _____ .

Dear God,
    Thanks for things to help me eat. Amen.

To the adult: *Encouraging your child to talk is one of the most important things you can do right now. Some children find it hard to tell what they are doing—that's why in this activity your child was encouraged to use real utensils. Sometimes it's hard to think and talk at the same time! And while your child learns to talk, you learn to listen. Now is the best time for your child to develop good verbal (or talking) skills and for you to develop attentive listening skills. You and your child will use these skills—in partnership—for many years. The talking-listening years are starting right now.*

Love is eternal.
1 Corinthians 13:8

Love Story

Instructions: Each time you read the word *love* in the story, give your child a hug or kiss.

Once upon a time there was a little child.
The child didn't know about Valentine's Day.
"Valentine's Day is a holiday of *love*,"
said his grandma.
"It's the day of *love*," said his brother.
"It's when people talk of *love*,"
said his mother.

"But what is *love*?" asked the little boy.
"I *love* you," said his grandma.
"I *love* you," said his brother.
"*Love* is warm cuddly feeling,"
said his mother.
"*Love* is what you feel when you
talk to Jesus."

Dear Jesus,
I love You. Amen.

To the adult: *What will you do when your child presents you with a genuine, child-made valentine? How do you respond? The correct response to any child's artwork is to be honest and positive. Samples: "I see you liked red." "Red is such a good color for Valentine's Day." "I can tell you worked so hard on this." "Tell me about this." Those are all appropriate responses for a young child and should be said "in love."*

Pray at all times.
1 Thessalonians 5:17

Nod, Shake, Turn, and Bow

I can nod my head "yes"
I can shake my head "no."
I can turn it one way
So very slow.

I'll now think inside
What to tell God today.
My head will bow down
Here as I pray.

Dear Jesus,
   I love You. Amen.

To the adult: *This verse offers an excellent way to settle a child down for prayer. You might want to mark the top of the page for easy reference. This also works well as a "lead-in" to meal-, nap- or nighttime prayers.*

He sends the wind.
Psalm 147:18

Blow, Wind, Blow

Instructions: Encourage your child to act out this verse.

God says to the March wind: "Blow, wind, blow.
Scrape away the winter snow. Blow, wind,
blow."

God says to the March wind: "Softly, move
softly. Let the buds burst on the trees.
Softly, move softly."

God says to the March wind: "Be a soft spring
breeze. Wave over the grass and trees.
Be a soft spring breeze."

God says to the March wind: "Stop, wait, shh!
Just whisper over river and hill; spring will
tiptoe in."

Dear Jesus,
For winds that blow and winds that sing,
thank You, God, for spring. Amen.

To the adult: *Flying a kite with a young child sounds like a great idea. But often, it's an idea before its time. Try this guaranteed kite. Take an empty plastic bread bag. Dump out the crumbs. Cut three holes near the top and tie a piece of yarn or string onto each hole. Make the strings about 12" long. Then your child can run with it!*

Watch for the new thing I am going to do.
Isaiah 43:19

Surprise!

Instructions: Encourage your child to act out each surprise.

Surprise!
A jack-in-the-box pops up.

Surprise!
I see baby birds in the nest. Tweet, tweet.

Surprise!
I blow away the dandelion fluff.

Surprise!
I blow out all the candles on the birthday cake.

Surprise!
The snowman melts.

Dear Jesus,
    You don't surprise me. I know You're my Jesus.
Amen.

To the adult: *The refrigerator door is a place for surprises to happen. The surface offers a great place to store magnets. Some families collect magnets from places they've visited. Other refrigerator magnets hold up children's artwork. Your child will love playing with magnets on the refrigerator: he'll be close to you in the kitchen and the "magnet board" is always at the right height for him. Don't put out all the magnets at any one time. Rotate magnets to build up an element of surprise!*

When Jesus was twelve years old, they
went to the festival as usual.
Luke 2:42

Jesus at Church

Instructions: Your child can respond with the words, "My Jesus," at the end of each line. This will give her a chance to help "tell" the story of Jesus in the Temple.

Jesus walked to church. (*My Jesus*)
He went with His parents. (*My Jesus*)
Then they couldn't find (*my Jesus*).
Mary asked, "Where is (*my Jesus?*")
Joseph asked, "Where is (*my Jesus?*")
Then Mary saw Him: ("*My Jesus!*")
Then Joseph saw Him: ("*My Jesus!*")
We, too, can say, "*My Jesus.*"

Dear Jesus,
I'm glad You always know where I am. Amen.

To the adult: *Play hide and seek using one of your child's larger toys.*

Lord, You have made so many things!
            Psalm 104:24

Squirrels

Instructions: Encourage your child to act out this verse, especially doing the fingerplay at the end.

> The furry squirrel peeks out her head.
> "God made this day; get out of bed!"
> The furry squirrel squeaks in the tree,
> "Come out, you little ones, with me."
> Now here they come: 1–2–3–4.
> They scamper out the tree's front door
> And bounce along the tree's big limb.
> The first one says, "Can I go in?"
> The second says, "It's fun up here."
> The third one says, "Oh, do not fear."
> The fourth one says, "I see God's world."
> And Mother says, "Thank God for squirrels."

Dear Jesus,
        My favorite animal is ⎯⎯⎯⎯ . Amen.

To the adult: *Large muscle development occurs before small muscle development. That is a basic fact of child growth. That's one of the reasons fingerplays, like this one, give such great small muscle practice to young children. A basic small muscle activity is stringing beads. Be sure the beads are large and the child has a well-tipped shoelace for stringing. After the young child strings several, tie a knot, so if the string falls, the child won't lose all the beads. Even in a simple activity like this, you'll want to do everything possible to let the child experience success.*

The wind blows wherever it wishes.
John 3:8

Blowin' in the Wind

Instructions: Encourage your child to use his arms and his mouth with this activity.

When a kite flies high, the wind blows like this
_____ .
When storm clouds gather, and lightening
flashes, the wind blows like this _____ .
When the rain is pouring down, the wind blows
like this _____ .
When the sun comes out after a storm, the wind
blows like this _____ .
Today the wind is blowing like this _____ .

_____

Dear Jesus,
When the wind blows hard I feel
_____ . Amen.

To the adult: *Children often delight in the wind. Wind blows hair across their faces and it tickles. Winds flap clothes and that's fun! Help your child notice wind: your child can wet the tip of a finger and point it toward the wind. Can your child catch the wind like that?*

Look at my hands.
Luke 24:39

Feely Fingers

Instructions: Encourage your child to move around the room for this activity.

My fingers can feel
  ♦ something soft. (How many things can you touch that are soft?)
  ♦ something hard. (How many things can you touch that feel hard?)
  ♦ something smooth. (How many things can you touch that feel smooth?)
My fingers can feel your fingers! (Hold hands with your child.)

———————

Dear Jesus,
  Thank You for my feely fingers. Amen.

To the adult: *Continue this game. Take an empty bag of any kind. Put in, one at a time, objects familiar to your child: a spoon, cup, washcloth. See if your child can name the object just by feeling. (No peeking!)*

I have cared for you from the time you
were born. Isaiah 46:3

Baby Days

Instructions: Encourage your child to act out each growth step.

When I was a baby
+ I slept.
+ I cried.
+ I learned to roll over.
+ I learned to sit up.
+ I learned to crawl.
+ I learned to stand up.
Now I can say:

_____

Dear Jesus,
Thank You for helping me grow up. Amen.

To the adult: *We often focus on the growth of our young child. But the little one isn't the only one who grows. Think back: How have you grown as a caregiver in the past months? God has blessed your growing, too.*

All living things look hopefully to You.
Psalm 145:15

Woof! Woof!

Instructions: Encourage your child to act out this verse.

Dogs like to dig.
They use their paws.
God gave dogs digging paws.

Dogs like to sniff.
They bury their bones.
God gave dogs sniffy noses.

Dogs like to wag.
They wag their tails.
God gave dogs waggy tails.

Dogs like to bark.
They say "woof, woof."
God gave dogs woofy voices.

I like to pray.
I talk to God and say:
Thank You, God, for dogs. Amen.

―――――――――――

To the adult: *Dogs can be big, noisy, and overly friendly. Those same things that appeal to older children may make younger children afraid. Young children commonly fear such animals. Gently introduce your child to dogs— perhaps using a stuffed animal or by visiting a pet shop.*

He is not here—He has been raised!
Mark 16:6

Happy Easter

Instructions: Help your child act out this verse.

A little springtime bunny goes *hop, hop, hop.*
A little springtime chick says *peep, peep, peep.*
A little child of God goes *clap, clap, clap.*
He's risen! He's risen! Jesus is alive.
Clap, clap, clap.

Dear Jesus,
    Thank You for being my Savior. Amen.

To the adult: *Look around the house with your child for signs of Easter.*

Through Him God created everything
in heaven and on earth.
                    Colossians 1:16

Balancing Acts

Instructions: Your child will need a washcloth for this activity.

I can balance a washcloth on my shoulder.
God gave me a great shoulder.

I can balance a washcloth on my head.
God gave me a great head.

I can balance a washcloth on my hand.
God gave me a great hand.

I can balance a washcloth on my foot.
God gave me a great body.

I can balance a washcloth on my tummy.
Whoops! I'm going to laugh!

————————

Dear Jesus,
        Thanks for all my parts. Amen.

To the adult: *This is a great time of year to make a beanbag for your child. Simply sew two washcloths together, using dry beans for stuffing. On a dry day outdoors, your child can hide the beanbag, play catch with you, or do balancing acts.*

You soften the soil with showers and
cause the young plants to grow.
Psalm 65:10

Here Comes Spring

Instructions: Stand outside or look out a window as you do this with your child.

I see a sign of spring.
It flies. It hunts for worms. It says "tweet, tweet."
It is a _____ .

I hear a sign of spring.
It goes "drip, drop." It makes splashy puddles.
It is _____ .

I feel a sign of spring.
It makes the trees blow. It keeps kites up in the sky.
It is _____ .

I see a sign of spring.
It is green. It pushes out of the ground.
It is _____ .

———————————

Dear Jesus,
Thank You for spring. Amen.

To the adult: *Children and adults are usually so glad to get out of the house in spring, it's easy to miss some of the beauty. This spring, take time to help your child observe. Look at the buds on a tree branch, at a drop of rain plunking in a puddle, at the first dandelion in the lawn. Looking closely at the miracles of spring helps us to focus on the majesty of God, our Creator.*

He has been raised.
Luke 24:6

1, 2, 3

Instructions: Encourage your child to use her fingers for this verse. There are some trick spots, so encourage your child to listen carefully.

1, 2, 3
Jesus rose for me.
3, 4, 5
Jesus is alive.
5, 6, 7
Jesus reigns in heaven.
8, 9, 10
It's Easter time again.
Hallelujah!

———————

Dear Jesus,
I'm glad You rose on Easter. Amen.

To the adult: *This type of rhyme is more difficult than simple finger counting. Older ones will delight in the challenge. Help younger ones with the activity so they feel good about their actions, too.*

Learn what I teach you.
Proverbs 2:1

Do This, Do That

Instructions: Here's an activity verse for your child.

Put your two hands on your head;
Then reach way up high.

Put your hands down at your sides
And stretch up to the sky.

Put your feet all tight together;
Now jump 1–2–3.

We'll end with hands together
So you can pray with me.

Dear Jesus,
Thank You for this time together. Amen.

To the adult: *This "Simon says" technique also works well when your child needs to get dressed or pick up the toys. Make chores into a game, and they'll get done faster.*

God is our shelter and strength.
Psalm 46:1

Moving

Instructions: Encourage your child to act out this verse.

People move to a new house.
They pack boxes. Pack, pack, pack.
And God goes with them.

People move to a new house.
They load boxes into a van. Load, load, load.
And God goes with them.

People move to a new house.
They drive the moving van. Drive, drive, drive.
And God goes with them.

People move to a new house.
They unpack the boxes. Unpack, unpack,
    unpack.
And God goes with them.

People move to a new house.
They shake hands with new friends. Shake,
    shake, smile!
And God goes with them.

———————

Dear Jesus,
    I'm glad You're always with me. Amen.

To the adult: *Moving to a new place can be a bother to an adult. Moving to a new place can alternately mean excitement and fun, and outright fear for a child. A child who moves gets tremendous comfort from familiar routines like daily devotions and prayers. During a move, keep basic living patterns as normal as possible, and always give thanks to God for His help in getting you through another day!*

You created every part of me.
Psalm 139:13

All Around a Chair

Instructions: Pull a chair into the middle of the room to help your child participate in this verse.

> I can crawl under the chair.
> Look at me go under.
> God gave me a great body.
>
> I can walk around the chair.
> Look at me go around.
> God gave me a great body.
>
> I can walk backwards around the chair.
> Look at me go around backwards.
> God gave me a great body.
>
> I can sit on the chair.
> Look at me on top.
> Now hear me pray:

> Dear Jesus,
> Thank You for all the ways I can move. Amen.

To the adult: *Early childhood educators identify learning spatial relationships as a goal young children should achieve. One aspect of that concept is understanding what some prepositions really mean. "Going round," "under," and "on top of" are things a child learns through daily activities, not by circling pictures in a workbook. Give your child every opportunity to have fun experimenting with these words using the great body God has given.*

Be glad . . . because of your Creator.
Psalm 149:2

Sounds of Spring

Instructions: Help your child act out this verse.

A lawn mower mows.
A bee goes buzz.
(*Clap!*)
God gave me spring.

A bird goes tweet.
A hose squirts water.
(*Clap!*)
God gave me spring.

The warm wind whispers.
The raindrops plunk.
(*Clap!*)
God gave me spring.

———————————

Dear Jesus,
I hear spring when ——————— . Amen.

To the adult: *Spring brings so many delights to children, they often miss the sounds. Stop for a moment. Listen to spring. What sounds can your child identify?*

Praise Him with drums.
Psalm 150:4

A Jesus Drum

Instructions: Give your child an empty coffee can, oatmeal container, or kitchen pot. Then help your child use his drum.

Rum-dee-dum
Rum-dee-dum.
I can play my Jesus drum.

Rum-dee-dum
Rum-dee-dum.
I march with my Jesus drum.

Rum-dee-dum
Rum-dee-dum
Listen to my Jesus drum.

_____

Dear Jesus,
I like to talk to You. Amen.

To the adult: *Your child can decorate a "Jesus drum" that can be used again. Simply ask your child to color on a piece of paper. Tape it around the pot or container used for this activity. Next time you feel a need to change the mood, bring out the Jesus drum.*

*Remember your Creator while you are
still young.*   Ecclesiastes 12:1

Swing into Spring

Instructions: Encourage your child to act out this verse.

My arms can swing.
My voice can sing:
Thank You, God, for spring.

My arms can swing.
My legs can swing.
My voice can sing:
Thank You, God, for spring.

My arms can swing.
My legs can swing.
My body swings.
My voice can sing:
Thank You, God, for spring.

Dear Jesus,
    Thank You for spring. Amen.

To the adult: *Poets say God's earth wakes up in spring. Twelve months makes
a big difference to a child. Last spring, your child couldn't—developmentally—
enjoy spring as she does this year. What a difference a year makes! And what
a difference spring makes! Enjoy the earth's outdoors with your young child.*

Everything that happens in this world
happens at the time God chooses.
Ecclesiastes 3:1

The Spring Robin

Instructions: Sing this with your child to the tune of "Farmer in the Dell."

Verse 1
The robin found a worm.
The robin found a worm.
Hooray! God gives us spring.
The robin found a worm.

Verse 2
The robin builds a nest.

Verse 3
The baby birdies "tweet."

Dear Jesus,
    I like to sing.
    Thank You for spring. Amen.

To the adult: *Encourage your child to make up his own verses to this song.*

He will . . . guide our steps into the
path of peace.   Luke 1:79

Neat Feet

Instructions: Have your child go barefoot for this activity.

> God gave me feet
>> So I can walk around.
> God gave me feet
>> As I tiptoe, not a sound.
> God gave me feet
>> That I can wiggle, wiggle, wiggle.
> God gave me feet
>> That someone can tickle!

> Dear Jesus,
>> Thanks for my neat feet. Amen.

To the adult: *While your child is barefoot, trace around her feet. Have her stand with heels touching. Add a few antennae, and she'll have her own butterfly feet to color.*

God loves the one who gives gladly.
2 Corinthians 9:7

Money, Money

Instructions: Drop loose change into a little bag. Your child can shake it every time you say the words, "Money, money."

Coins make noise. (*Money, money.*)
Coins are heavy. (*Money, money.*)
Coins pay the doctor. (*Money, money.*)
Coins help children (*Money, money.*)
Learn about Jesus. (*Money, money.*)
Let's take coins (*Money, money.*)
To church on Sunday. (*Money, money.*)

Dear Jesus,
Thanks for money to give at church. Amen.

To the adult: *After your child is beyond the risk of swallowing coins, give your child many opportunities to touch coins. They can be sorted by color and kind. Also give your child the chance to learn how to make change. A fun way of doing this is to put price tags (1¢, 5¢, 10¢) on food cans in the pantry. Then play store. If you do this after shopping, your child can even help by putting groceries away on your shelves!*

When I was a child, my speech,
feelings, and thinking were all those
of a child.   1 Corinthians 13:11

Babytimes

Instructions: Encourage your child to act this out.

When I was just a little babe, I lived inside my
bed.
I slept and slept and slept and slept; I could not
lift my head.
But soon I looked around to see this world that
God has made.
I saw some people, colors, movements, dark
and light and shade.
I learned to roll from front to back, and then
the other way.
It seemed I learned at least a single brand-new
thing each day.
But that was, oh, so long ago, and now I'm all
grown up;
I feed myself, know how to eat, and drink right
from a cup.
And even though I'm now so big, each day I
spend some time
To thank my family and my Lord who helped
me grow up fine.

Dear Jesus,
Thank You for helping me grow. Amen.

To the adult: *Putting items in order by size is an early learning skill. Your child can do this easily by lining up items beginning with the smallest and ending with the largest. Outdoors, your child can make a line of sticks, stones, or anything that is safe for play and will show progression of size. Very young children might say, "This is the baby stick, the sister stick, and the mommy stick" or use similar words to understand the concept of big, bigger, biggest.*

The Lord is risen indeed!
Luke 24:34

An Easter Child

Instructions: Encourage your child to act out this verse.

> I'm an Easter child.
> I can clap my hands.
> Jesus is alive.

> I'm an Easter child.
> I can lift my shoulders.
> Jesus is alive.

> I'm an Easter child.
> I can blink my eyes.
> Jesus is alive.

> I'm an Easter child.
> I can nod my head.
> Jesus is alive.

> Dear Jesus,
> Thank You for making Easter. Amen.

To the adult: *The concept of Easter is almost impossible for a young child to understand. Very young children can simply be told we have Easter to celebrate that "Jesus is alive."*

Teach a child how he should live.
Proverbs 22:6

Church Time

Instructions: Encourage your child to act out this verse.

I like to go to church
Where I can sing and pray.
But I won't roller skate to church;
At least I won't today!

I like to go to church
Where I can sing and pray.
But I won't ride a bike to church;
At least I won't today!

I like to go to church where
I can sing and pray.
But I won't fly a kite to church;
At least I won't today.

I like to go to church
Where I can sing and pray.
But I won't jump a rope to church;
At least I won't today!

———————————

Dear Jesus,
I'm glad I can go to church. Amen.

To the adult: *Too often, parents of young children go to church hoping to "survive" another Sunday morning. Do everything you can to ensure your own personal joyful worship. For example, start Sunday morning on Saturday night by setting out the breakfast dishes and laying out church clothes for you and your child. Plan ahead, too, how your child will be occupied so you have time to dress. Consider using a short video from the local Christian bookstore or an Arch Books Aloud!®.*

*Praise Him . . . all animals, tame and
wild, reptiles and birds.*
Psalm 148:9–10

Blanket Butterfly

Instructions: For this activity, your child can crawl under a bath towel or
blanket. Encourage your child to act out the life cycle of the butterfly. For a
really great caterpillar, you can crawl underneath, too!

God makes a butterfly happen, in a special way.
He has it live as a caterpillar, for many, many
days.
It squiggles forward, squiggles back, like a big
fat worm.
It wiggles all around and makes a flip-flop kind
of turn.
(*Wiggle under blanket.*)

When God says, "The time is up," it spins a nice
cocoon
Where it's all quiet, dark, and cozy, like a little
room.
(*Stay quiet under blanket.*)

But God knows best and is in charge of every
living thing.
So one day the skin goes "crack"; a butterfly
sees spring.
(*Pop up from blanket.*)

———————————

Dear Jesus,
    Thanks for pretty butterflies. Amen.

To the adult: *Your child can make a "caterpillar salad." Just have him arrange
grapes or melon balls in a squiggly line on a lettuce leaf.*

Come, let us bow down and
worship Him.   Psalm 95:6

I Can Count

Instructions: Encourage your child to count along with the verse.

God gave me knees;
I'll count up to two.
God gave me eyes
Just to see you.

God gave me fingers;
I'll count up to ten.
God gave me toes.
I'll count ten again!

I've only one nose;
That's where I smell.
With all of these parts
(See?) God made me well.

Dear Jesus,
        Thanks for hands to fold when I pray. Amen.

To the adult: *Help your child focus on different body parts by using easy-to-make binoculars. Simply tape together two empty toilet paper rolls. What can your child see?*

As long as the world exists, there will
be a time for planting.   Genesis 8:22

Happy Spring!

Instructions: Say the words on each line, then ask your child to echo them.
Begin very, very softly. End up with a loud *Happy Spring!*

Springtime is (*Springtime is*)
Coming soon. (*coming soon.*)
Look for flowers (*Look for flowers*)
That will bloom. (*that will bloom.*)
God made spring (*God made spring*)
With skies so blue. (*with skies so blue.*)
God made spring (*God made spring*)
For me and you. (*for me and you.*)
Happy Spring!

Dear Jesus,
        Thank You for the springtime. Amen.

To the adult: *Tossing confetti is one of the easiest ways to express a celebration spirit. Ask your child to color a paper using spring colors. Then she can cut pieces, any shape or size. (If your child is just learning to cut, hold a piece of paper for your child while she goes "open close, open close" with the scissors. One of the tricks of successful cutting for a young child is to hold the paper for the child.) Using your child's own version of confetti, read this echo verse again. Your child can toss the confetti for Happy Spring. Chances are great that your child will eagerly clean up the confetti—just to do the verse with you again!*

The Lord created the earth.
Proverbs 3:19

Crawl Around

Instructions: Encourage your child to act this out.

I can crawl like a snake, slither on the ground.
I can crawl like a worm, on the sidewalk,
all around.
I can crawl like a caterpillar who'll soon fly
away.
I can crawl like a baby, for I used to move
that way.
All these crawling, creeping creatures, were
made by God above.
He created them and keeps them in His holy
love.

Dear Jesus,
Thanks for making me. Amen.

To the adult: *Crawling is one of the most common actions we can observe in the play of young children. When you watch your child at play during the next few weeks, notice how often he naturally moves on his stomach.*

The earth is filled with Your creatures.
Psalm 104:24

Wake Up!

Instructions: Encourage your child to act out this verse.

What wakes up in spring?

Bears wake up. They stretch and stretch.

Snakes wake up. They slither around.

Bees wake up. They buzz, buzz.

Beavers wake up. They slap, slap.

A beautiful spring day dawns. The sun shines.
The breeze blows gently.
The owl says "hoot, hoot" and goes back to
sleep.

———————————

Dear Jesus,
Thanks for the signs of spring. Amen.

To the adult: *Help your child uncover some of the animals of spring. Turn over a leaf, a rock, a log. Prepare your child in advance—a young child might be frightened, or delighted, to see all the scurrying once the cover is removed from an animal's hiding place.*

*You send abundant rain on
the plowed fields.*   Psalm 65:10

Pitter Pat

Instructions: Have your child tap fingers on a table and say "pitter pat" as indicated.

> Rain drops. (*Pitter pat.*)
> Water flowers. (*Pitter pat.*)
> Wash the cars. (*Pitter pat.*)
> Bathe the birds. (*Pitter pat.*)
> Clean the streets. (*Pitter pat.*)
> Make some puddles. (*Pitter pat.*)
> Splash, splash, splash. (*Pitter pat.*)

> Dear Jesus,
>   Thanks for rain. Amen.

To the adult: *After a spring rain, while the sidewalks are still wet, give your child some colored chalk. Your child's drawings will be vivid in color and wash off easily with the next rain.*

In the countryside the flowers
are in bloom.   Song of Songs 2:12

Flowers

Instructions: Encourage your child to act out this story as you read the words.

Before there is a flower, there is a tiny seed.
I dig a hole and drop it in.
Where is my flower now?

Before there is a flower, God makes the rain-
drops fall.
I watch the drops go pitter pat.
Where is my flower now?

Before there is a flower, God makes the sun
shine bright.
I watch the shadows play.
Where is my flower now?

Look! Now I see a flower. God sends the sun
and rain.
My flower is so pretty
I'll go back and plant again.

Dear Jesus,
    Thanks for Your pretty flowers. Amen.

To the adult: *This is an easy story for your child to act out for friends or relatives. Having a young child informally share this kind of "story" can contribute to building a good feeling about himself.*

The winter is over.
Song of Songs 2:11

An In-Out Day

Instructions: Give your child a small towel for this activity. Whenever a line begins with *Whoops!* she can hide underneath the towel.

The day is started; I'll go out to play.
Whoops! There's a cloud. It's an in-out day.

The cloud has flown. It's far away.
Whoops! There's another. It's an in-out day.

The sun is bright; now I can play.
Whoops! Time to eat! It's an in-out day.

Back and forth, I know it's May.
Whoops! It's the month for in-out days.

———————————

Dear Jesus,
Wherever I am, I know You're with me. Amen.

To the adult: *Before the hot weather—now!—is the best time to be sure your child will have a shady outdoor play area. Children's internal thermometers don't regulate as well as adults'. They can get overheated without being aware of it. Putting the sandbox in the shade, or having a corner to dig under a tree can make a safer, happier summer.*

You provide food, and they are satisfied. Psalm 104:28

Finger Foods

Instructions: Have your child show the shape of each finger food mentioned.

Of all the foods God gives me
The ones I like the most
Are apples, crunchy carrot sticks,
And, in the morning, toast.

You see these foods are special;
I eat them by myself.
So I thank God for finger foods
That are good for my health.

———————————

Dear Jesus,
   I like to eat ——————————— . Amen.

To the adult: *One standard finger food for young children is a sandwich. The next time you serve one to your child, use a cookie cutter to cut out the bread, meat, and cheese. A shapely sandwich will be lots of fun to eat!*

*The air is fragrant with blossoming
vines.*   Song of Songs 2:13

Buzz, Buzz

Instructions: Encourage your child to count on five fingers for this fingerplay.

The first little bee flew out of the hive.
The second one buzzed, "Thank God I'm alive."
The third little bee buzzed off to some clover.
The fourth little bee said, "Please move over."
The fifth little bee looked 'round to say, "Thank
You, God, for this beautiful day."

———————————

Dear Jesus,
On this early summer day,
Thanks for this weather is what I say. Amen.

To the adult: *Some young children have difficulty learning the ordinals, or numerical positions. There is nothing to suggest that learning the concepts "first, second, third," is really difficult. Often, we just don't make a point of labeling items in this way. Next time you are counting silverware or lining up shoes, simply say, "This is the first, second . . . ." This is an easy way to let your child expand his basic understanding of 1, 2, 3.*

He breathed life-giving breath into . . .
the man. Genesis 2:7

I Can Blow It!

Instructions: Encourage your child to act out this verse.

I can blow it!
Watch me blow a dandelion.

I can blow it!
Watch me blow a pinwheel.

I can blow it!
Watch me blow a trumpet.

I can blow it!
Watch me blow bubbles.

Dear Jesus,
For air that I can blow
And eyes that see things go,
Thank You, Jesus. Amen.

To the adult: *Look through a magazine with your child. Help him find pictures of things that might move with the wind.*

[God's] love is so great that we are
called God's children.   1 John 3:1

Sayings

Instructions: Have your child answer the questions.

> Who says:
> ◆ Oink, oink?
> ◆ Let's eat?
> ◆ Tweet, tweet?
> ◆ I love you?
> Jesus loves you, too!

> Dear Jesus,
> I love You. Amen.

To the adult: *A young child experiences the love of Christ through people like you. The way you care, forgive, and share is one way Jesus' love touches the young. Our Lord is working through you to touch the life of the child with whom you share this book. Thanks be to Him!*

Come, let us praise the Lord!
Psalm 95:1

Going to Church

Instructions: Encourage the child to act out this verse.

When I go to church I sing, sing, sing.
God gave me a voice to praise Him.

When I go to church I smile, smile, smile.
God gave me a mouth to show joy.

When I go to church I hold another hand.
God gave me hands to bring others.

When I go to church I pray, pray, pray.
God is always near to listen.

Dear Jesus,
Thank You for my church. Amen.

To the adult: *Does your child have a friend who could be invited to church? Offer to take the child with you. Your young one might be on best behavior by bringing a friend, and you'll be planting the concept of being Jesus' helper.*

Let the earth produce all kinds of
animal life.   Genesis 1:24

Animals, Animals

Instructions: Encourage your child to act out this verse.

A bear in the forest might sleep in a cave.
That's no pet for me.
A lion in the grasslands might roar aloud.
That's no pet for me.
A monkey in the jungle might climb a tree.
That's no pet for me.
God made cats and dogs so soft and warm to
hug.
Now those are pets for me.

———————————

Dear Jesus,
I like some animals like ——————— . Amen.

To the adult: *Pick up a copy of the newspaper. With your child, look for a picture of an animal. Talk about whether or not it would make a good pet.*

Be glad, fields and everything in you!
Psalm 96:12

Yum, Yum

Instructions: Before starting this devotion, stop at the refrigerator. Select several fruits or vegetables, each of a different color. Set the food on the table in front of your child and play this guessing game.

God gives us food to eat that's green.
What do you see that's green?

God gives us food to eat that's yellow.
What do you see that's yellow?

God gives us food to eat that's red.
What do you see that's red?

God gives us food that you like to eat.
What is your favorite food?

———————

Dear Jesus,
Thank You for good things to eat. Amen.

To the adult: *Encourage your child to group the foods on the table in different ways: things that grow under the ground; foods that some animals like, too. Do this only if your child seems to enjoy (and be ready for) this activity.*

Be happy while you are still young.
Ecclesiastes 11:9

Legwork

Instructions: For this activity, have your child lie on his back on a carpet.

Let's pretend; kick your legs in the air
like you are
♦ swimming
♦ jumping
♦ walking

Now let's do everything again, right side up!

Dear Jesus,
I'm learning to move in so many ways,
Thank you, Jesus, for these great days. Amen.

To the adult: *Informally introduce your child to hopping on one foot and jumping with two feet. Wait, though, with skipping. Skipping is a complicated activity which some children—especially boys—don't learn until the age of 6, 7, or even later.*

Let the children come to Me.
Luke 18:16

Puppet Talk

Instructions: For this devotion, make a paper bag puppet. Take an empty brown bag and draw a simple face onto the bottom. Let the puppet tell this story. Fill in the blanks with names that mean the most to your child.

> Hi! My name is Baggy. I came to your house,
> right here on _____ Street, to
> tell you about Jesus. You know about Jesus.
> He knows about you, _____ .
> Jesus is your Savior. One of the places you
> learn about Jesus is at _____
> Church. I know one of your favorite people
> there is _____ . You can learn
> about Jesus right here, though, too. Do you
> know where the Bible is kept? Ask someone
> to read to you about when little children
> came to see Jesus. Bye-bye for now. Can
> you wave to me?

Dear Jesus,
> Thank You for the Bible. Amen.

To the adult: *Let your child have some puppet fun, too. A mismatched sock makes a good puppet for a young child. Draw a face on the sock with a marking pen. Your child's puppet can talk to "Baggy."*

Be glad, earth and sky!
Psalm 96:11

I See and Hear

Instructions: Encourage children to make the appropriate sounds and do the appropriate actions.

In summer I hear a dog bark. I see a tail wag.
In summer I hear a church bell ring.
    I see people walking.
In summer I hear a mower start. I see the
    grass get cut.
In summer I hear a siren whine. I see people
    getting help.
In summer I hear, "Let's go swimming."
    I run for my swimsuit!

Dear Jesus,
    Thanks for my ears that hear and my eyes
    that see. Amen.

To the adult: *You and your child can try listening for this summer sound. Put your ear to the grass. Get as close as possible. Now someone else can walk up to the person on the ground. Can the person hear the footsteps?*

Listen to the noise.

Isaiah 13:4

Animal Talk

Instructions: Help your child act out this verse.

Buzz, buzz, buzz.
God made a bee.
I buzz, too.
Listen to me.

Meow, meow, meow.
God made a cat.
I meow, too.
Listen to that.

Talk, talk, talk.
God made me.
I can talk.
Thanks, God, for me.

———————

Dear Jesus,
I can make all different kinds of noises. Amen.

To the adult: *What other animal sounds can your child identify? Make one sound at a time to see if your child can name which animal moos, quacks, neighs, and says hee-haw.*

He fills my life with good things.
Psalm 103:5

See 'N' Tell

Instructions: Play this word game with your child.

I'm looking for something we sit on. What do I see?

I'm looking for something that turns on. What do I see?

I'm looking for someone Jesus forgives. Whom do I see?

I'm looking for something we walk on. What do I see?

I'm looking for someone Jesus loves. Whom do I see?

I'm looking for something that gets hot. What do I see?

I'm looking for someone who loves Jesus. Whom do I see?

Dear Jesus,
Thank You for _____ . Amen.

To the adult: *Use this game in the car. Play it with different categories of items: things God gives to help us move around; animals God made, etc.*

He has set the right time for
everything.   Ecclesiastes 3:11

Tick Tock

Instructions: For this activity, you and your child can pretend to be a clock pendulum. Stand straight, with hands at your sides. Act out the pendulum movement by stepping on one foot and then the other, back and forth.

> Time to get up.
> Time for today.
> Time now to eat.
> Time now to play.
> Time to go out.
> Time to go here.
> Time to go in.
> Time to go there.
> Time to slow down.
> The end of a day.
> Time to pray:

> Dear Jesus,
> Thank You for this summer day—
> for all I did, thank You, I pray. Amen.

To the adult: *The pattern of a typical day can give a child a sense of security. This is especially important when seasons—and perhaps schedules, too—change. But some things stay the same: getting dressed, mealtimes, and Jesus time.*

Their angels in heaven . . . are always
in the presence of My Father.
Matthew 18:10

Summer Sleepovers

Instructions: Have your child repeat the last line in each stanza.

We might sleep in a cabin
On a summer trip.
But we aren't all alone:
Jesus sends His angels.

We might sleep in a tent
On a summer trip.
But we aren't all alone:
Jesus sends His angels.

We might sleep in a hotel
On a summer trip.
But we aren't all alone:
Jesus sends His angels.

We might sleep in a (child fills in)
On a summer trip.
But we aren't all alone:
Jesus sends His angels.

Dear Jesus,
Thank You for sending me an angel. Amen.

To the adult: *The concept of a guardian angel is certainly comforting to a parent. Children, too, can feel God's presence through His "messenger," which is what the word means. Talk about today's Scripture reading with your young child. Your child will probably draw a mental picture of "her" angel.*

You show Your care for the land.
Psalm 65:9

Four Seasons

Instructions: Help your child act out this verse.

There are four seasons of the year:
Fall, winter, spring, and summer.
I can count them on my fingers
And they are four in number.

In fall the temperature gets cool.
I put on warmer clothes
For winter will be coming soon
As everybody knows.

The earth sleeps soundly, then wakes up.
Birds build their nests and sing:
Peep, peep, peep, peep, peep, peep, peep, peep.
"Cheer up!" It's time for spring.

Now summer time is finally here,
We can look back and say:
God made the seasons. Thank You, Lord,
Today and every day.

Dear Jesus,
Thank You for summer. Amen.

To the adult: *Learning about seasons is an abstract concept for young children. They will learn most easily about yearly changes when you talk and do different things in the different seasons. For example, children might associate spring with "my birthday," summer with swimming, and winter with Jesus' birthday.*

Your greatness is seen in all the world.
                    Psalm 8:9

Let's Hike

Instructions: *As you read this verse, stand up with your child and pretend to go on a walk together. Hold hands if that seems natural.*

I'm going on a hike.
I might see something that blooms.
That might be a _____ and God
    made it.

I'm going on a hike.
I might see something with four legs.
That might be a _____ and God
    made it.

I'm going on a hike.
I might see something with pretty wings.
That might be a _____ and God
    made it.

Dear Jesus,
    Thank You for this pretty world. Amen.

To the adult: *A walk down the street can be turned into a kid-sized hike. Take a plastic container of juice and trail mix (round cereal, raisins, and mini-marshmallows) in a baggie. Add a bathroom towel (for sitting under a tree) and a compass or flashlight, if desired.*

A gentle answer quiets anger.
Proverbs 15:1

I Can Hear You!

Instructions: Have your child mimic your words.

Say loudly:
I love you. (child repeats)
Jesus loves you. (child repeats)

Say in a normal tone of voice:
I love you. (child repeats)
Jesus loves you. (child repeats)

Whisper:
I love you. (child repeats)
Jesus loves you. (child repeats)

Whisper the prayer:

_____

Dear Jesus,
Thank You for loving me. Amen.

To the adult: *The next time you feel like yelling at your child, try a whisper instead. Soft voices—which force children to pay attention—can be more effective than loud voices. Really!*

The hillsides are full of joy.
Psalm 65:12

What Do Flowers Say?

Instructions: Make two facial tissue "talking flowers." Simply crumple a tissue into a tight ball and cover it with another. Loosely wrap a rubber band around the "neck" of the flower. Make it loose enough to wear over your finger. Do the same thing with the second flower. Draw a simple face. Place one flower on your child's finger, another on yours:

Adult's flower says:
The sun shines so bright. I want to smile.
Child's flower says:
Thank You God, for summer.
Adult's flower says:
The rain is so wet. I want to smile.
Child's flower says:
Thank You, God, for summer.
Adult's flower says:
The breeze is so warm. I want to smile.
Child's flower says:
Thank You, God, for summer.

Dear Jesus,
Thank You for summer. Amen.

To the adult: *Your child might want to continue using the puppets long after this devotion. Listen carefully to what the puppets "say." Children sometimes talk in a "second-hand" way, for example through puppets, about things they might not otherwise discuss in their own person.*

Play drums . . . in praise of Him.
Psalm 149:3

A Jesus Parade

Instructions: Your child will need a pot and spoon for this activity. You can have a parade. Your child can "play drums" marching around the room while you read the verse:

March 2-3-4
March 2-3-4
I love Jesus.
I love Jesus.
March 2-3-4
March 2-3-4
Jesus loves me.
Jesus loves me.

Dear Jesus,
I love You. Amen.

To the adult: *Your child can enjoy banging an upside-down pan with a spoon. This is a great activity while you are in the kitchen preparing a meal. A large plastic spoon makes less noise than one of metal.*

Come, let us praise the Lord!
Psalm 95:1

Let's Go to Church

Instructions: This is an adaptation of the popular children's clapping game, "We're going on a bear hunt." Simply slap your thighs at each italicized word. This is most fun if you and your child sit cross-legged on the floor facing each other.

We're *going for* a *car* ride.
Get *in* the *car* now.
Let's *go* to *church*.
We're *going for* a *car* ride.
Fasten the *seat* belt.
Let's *go* to *church*.
We're *going for* a *car* ride.
Bumpety—bumpety—bump.
Let's *go* to *church*.
We're *done* with our *ride*.
We'll *sing* and *pray*.
Let's *go* to *church*.

Dear Jesus,
Thank You for my church. Amen.

To the adult: *Going to church with a young child isn't always easy. But regular worship participation demonstrates to children the importance you place on going to church. And church-going is more than just a good tradition, after all. Your child will grow up knowing that church is a happy place to learn about Jesus.*

Nothing can hide from [the sun's]
heat. Psalm 19:6

Hot Weather

Instructions: Encourage your child to act out these lines.

It's so hot today,
An ice cream cone would melt.
Drip, drip, drip, right into my mouth.

It's so hot today,
A Popsicle™ would melt.
Drip, drip, drip, right into my mouth.

It's so hot today,
An ice cube would melt.
Drip, drip, drip, right into my mouth.

———————————

Dear Jesus,
Thanks for cold foods that melt on hot days. Amen.

To the adult: *Children naturally want to be outside in water on hot summer days. A bath, complete with bubbles, offers a welcome retreat from the sun. You might enjoy one, too! But, of course, it might look so inviting, your child will want to join you.*

Trust in the Lord, rely on your God.
Isaiah 50:10

Vacation

Instructions: Act out these verses with sound effects.

I'm on vacation in a car.
I sit, sit, sit.
Jesus comes along with me.
Honk! Honk! Honk!

I'm on vacation in a plane.
I fly, fly, fly.
Jesus comes along with me.
Zoom! Zoom! Zoom!

I'm on vacation in a train.
I go bumpety, bumpety, bump.
Jesus comes along with me.
Whoo! Whoo! Whoo!

I'm on vacation in a boat.
I splash, splash, splash.
Jesus comes along with me.
Varoom, varoom, varoom.

Dear Jesus,
I'm glad You're always with me. Amen.

To the adult: *Finding devotional time on vacation can be as challenging as finding devotional time at home. It's easiest to simply add a few minutes onto a daily activity, that you'd do wherever you are. A few minutes after supper, or before brushing teeth at night, or whenever you normally plan devotions also gives your child the security of a familiar routine.*

I am the One who created you.
Isaiah 44:24

Farm Animals

Instructions: Encourage your child to make sounds for the different animals.

A rooster crows "cock-a-doodle do."
A cow gives out a great big "moo."
A chicken in a coop goes "cluck."
You know at a "quack," that it's a duck.
Who made animals "quack," "cluck," and "moo"?
God gave them voices. That's who!

———————————

Dear Jesus,
Thank You for animals. Amen.

To the adult: *Young children are often afraid the first time they see live farm animals. To get an idea of just how large a horse or cow appears to a young child, crouch in front of the animal. Then you will be about the same height as a 2- or 3-year-old. No wonder a horse looks so big—it is!*

He turns darkness into daylight.
                    Amos 5:8

Wake Up!

Instructions: Encourage your child to act out this verse.

On mornings when I am asleep,
    all cozy tucked in bed,
I try to stay there, sound asleep,
    not even lift my head.
But light is showing from outside;
    I see it 'round my door.
So even though it's early yet,
    I jump onto the floor.
I stretch my arms, my legs, and toes;
    I shake my fingers, too.
God gave a brand-new day to me
    and there is much to do.
"Wake up, wake up," I call out loud.
    "God gave us a new day."
"Get up, get up," I call about.
    "Get up and start this day."

———————————

Dear Jesus,
    Thank You for today. Amen.

To the adult: *Young children often wake up earlier than their parents would hope. Also, young children often think, "If I'm up, everyone else should be, too." As soon as your child can play safely and independently, plan some "morning only" toys. Get them out the night before. Talk to your child about using them in the morning. Be sure "morning toys" are put away before breakfast for use another morning.*

Shout for joy, you heavens! Shout,
deep places of the earth. Isaiah 44:23

Under, On, Above

Instructions: Do this activity where your child can be underneath something for the first part, stand up for the second part, and be on top of something for the third part before coming back to earth. A chair (standing on it just this once with your support!) or bed will work, although ideally your child could build a tunnel to go under, and a flat of blocks to climb onto.

(Your child is underneath something.)
God made things under the ground:
- worms that wiggle
- carrots that grow down
- moles that tunnel

(Your child stands up.)
God made things on the ground:
- trees that blow in the wind
- dogs that wag their tails
- sunflowers that grow so tall

(Your child stands on top of something.)
God made things above the ground:
- stars that twinkle
- birds that fly
- rain that falls

(Your child gets down.)
God made many things. And God made me!

Dear Jesus,
Thanks for making so many neat things. Amen.

To the adult: *A life preserver easily demonstrates the "under, on, above" concepts to a child. Your child might enjoy "rescuing" toy animals or dolls with a paper preserver. Simply cut a "donut" from a brown paper bag. For a child-sized vest-type play preserver, cut down the length of a large brown paper bag, cut a round hole in the bottom and a round hole on each side.*

Look how the wild flowers grow.
Matthew 6:28

Flower Time

Instructions: Encourage your child to "be" a flower and act out this verse.

The summer flowers stand up high
To stretch their necks and reach the sky.
They close up tight when day is done.
They open only for the sun.

When God sends rain their heads droop low
As if to say, "Oh, yes, we know.
We need the rain. It feels so good.
God cares for us. We knew He would."

God sends to flowers rain and sun.
He cares for each, yes, every one.
And we can feel this same way, too:
God cares for me. He cares for you.

———————————

Dear Jesus,
Thank You for taking care of me
this summer. Amen.

To the adult: *This is a great time for a mid-summer safety check. In spring, adults who live around young children are usually exceptionally careful with weed trimmers, lawn equipment, and garden tools. By July though, it's easy to get a little careless. Carefully reexamine outdoor areas used by your young child. Also check tricycles and swings for loose bolts or bolt covers that have come off.*

God is the One who made the
mountains.   Amos 4:13

Climbing a Mountain

Instructions: Encourage your child to act out this verse.

I'm climbing up a mountain
To see what God has made.
I'm climbing up a mountain
Through sun and clouds and shade.

I'm climbing up a mountain.
My legs are getting sore.
I'm climbing up a mountain.
Oh! Now I can see more.

I'm finally on the mountain.
Look at what I see:
The trees! The sky! The rivers!
God's world for you and me.

Dear Jesus,
    Thank You for this wonderful world. Amen.

To the adult: *Look for "pretend" mountains for your young one to climb: a mound of laundry, a pile of dirt, etc. Your child can be encouraged to make his own mountain in the sandbox. Sticks can be trees; a piece of paper colored with blue crayon makes a lake.*

May the peoples praise You, O God.
Psalm 67:5

Going to a Fair

Instructions: Help your child act out the verses.

♦ Kiddie cars
The little cars they go so fast.
Zoom! Zoom! Zoom!
They speed up fast and faster still.
Varoom! Varoom! Varoom!

♦ Ferris wheel
The wheel I watch is very big.
It goes up to the sky.
My neck gets tired watching it,
The ferris wheel so high.

♦ The merry-go-round
Round and round and round I go
On the merry-go-round.
Round and round and round I go
And never touch the ground.

———————

Dear Jesus,
Thank You for people who take me to
fun places. Amen.

To the adult: *Going to a fair can be fun. For a young child, though, a fair can be downright scary. Balloons pop, rides are noisy, people can be dressed in costumes: all of these elements that can be enjoyable for older children can make young children fearful. Gently introduce your child to fairs—and then be ready to leave early if necessary.*

Sing a new song to Him.
Psalm 33:3

Sunday

Instructions: Sing this tune to "Here We Go 'Round the Mulberry Bush" while you hold hands with your child and act out the words.

Sunday is a special day, special day, special
day.
Sunday is a special day, when we can walk to
church.

Sunday is a special day, special day, special
day.
Sunday is a special day, when we can hop to
church.

Sunday is a special day, special day, special
day.
Sunday is a special day, when we can jump to
church.

Sunday is a special day, special day, special
day.
Sunday is a special day, when we can skip to
church.

Dear Jesus,
I'm glad to have a church to go to. Amen.

To the adult: *Use this little verse next Sunday morning while you're helping your child get ready for church. Simply substitute your own words in the last line, for example: "Sunday is a special day when we get dressed for church." Or, "Sunday is a special day; we comb your hair for church."*

Give us day by day the food we need.
Luke 11:3

That Tastes Great!

Instructions: Encourage your child to rub her tummy when she hears the name of a food she likes.

God gives me carrots.
God gives me ice cream.
God gives me oatmeal.
God gives me hamburgers.
God gives me cheese.
God gives me milk.
God gives me hot dogs.

Dear Jesus,
Thanks for foods that taste good. Amen.

To the adult: *It's not always easy to create nutritious foods that appeal to young children. Try these snacks: Cube cheese. Put a pretzel stick into each cube. Or buy plastic party toothpicks. Then let your child spear her own pineapple chunks. Use the same type of toothpick for a mini-fruit kebab. A toothpick will hold two pieces of fruit; grapes, banana slices, and melon balls work well. Watch your child closely while she eats from the toothpick.*

The sun will not hurt you
during the day.   Psalm 121:6

Keepin' Cool

What can I do on a hot summer day?
I can take a nap.
I can get all wet.
I can stay in the shade.
I can drink lemonade.
I can suck on some ice.
Ah—that will be nice.

Dear Jesus,
Thank You for things to help me keep cool.
Amen.

To the adult: *When a young child is out in the sun, a sunbonnet, baseball cap, or visor can help reduce the sun's glare in the child's eyes. A headcovering is especially important when a child is near water and can get a sunburned scalp fairly quickly from the reflection off the sand or water. (Remember, infants and very young children might not have the natural sun protection given by a full head of hair.)*

Children are a gift from the Lord.
Psalm 127:3

Between

Instructions: Encourage your child to act out this verse.

God put my elbows between my wrists and
shoulders.
God put my waist between my shoulders and
my hips.
God put my longest fingers between my thumbs
and pinkies.
God put my legs between my ankles and my
knees.
God put my face between my two ears.
God put my smile where everybody can see it!

Dear Jesus,
I like me. I like You. Amen.

To the adult: *A full length mirror is one of the most important pieces of furniture to a child. Children need to spend time looking at themselves, who they are, and how they appear. Young children grow so fast, and change so quickly. They need to be able to keep up, visually, with their own growth.*

Give thanks to the Lord Almighty.
Jeremiah 33:11

Round and Round

Instructions: After reading each line, your child can respond with "round and round" while making his hands circle around in the air.

Stroller wheels—*(round and round.)*
Car wheels—*(round and round.)*
Bike wheels—*(round and round.)*
Wagon wheels—*(round and round.)*
Bus wheels—*(round and round.)*
Tractor wheels—*(round and round.)*
They all turn—*(round and round.)*

Dear Jesus,
Thanks for things that go round and round.
Amen.

To the adult: *Help your child notice different kinds of wheels during the next few days. Look for wheels everywhere—you'll probably discover some in rather surprising places.*

[God] fashioned the earth and all that
lives there.   Isaiah 42:5

Summer Sounds

Instructions: Encourage your child to make appropriate sounds in the middle of this verse.

I look out the window.
What do I see?
God's summertime world
Calling to me.

I listen with care
And hear many a sound
For summertime noises
Are circling round.

♦ A lawn mower roars
♦ A dog barks loudly
♦ Leaves rustle softly
♦ A bird chirps sweetly.

I look out the window and what do I see?
God's summertime world calling to me.

Dear Jesus,
    I like to hear the sounds of summer. Amen.

To the adult: *Joining other children for play happens easily on summer days. But actual playing "with" others takes time and experience. Plant the seeds of sharing early: it takes two to seesaw, swinging is more fun when you swing next to someone else; etc. Be patient and positive.*

I am the One who made the earth.
Isaiah 45:12

Summer Quiet

Instructions: Encourage your child to act out the middle section of this verse and do it without a sound.

I stand at the window and what do I hear?
God's summertime world whispers so near.
Listen carefully or you won't hear a sound
For summertime's quiet as it circles around:

- ♦ An ice cube melts.
- ♦ A tadpole swims.
- ♦ A bird finds a worm.
- ♦ The grass grows.

I stand at the window and what do I hear?
God's summertime world whispers so near.

Dear Jesus,
Thank You for the softness of summer. Amen.

To the adult: *Playing with salt is a quiet activity on a summer day. Simply empty a salt shaker into an old shoe box. Your child can trace shapes and letters with his finger. When play is over, your child can put back the lid and put away the box. This is a great way to practice independent skills.*

Sing, heavens! Shout for joy, earth!
Isaiah 49:13

The Park

Instructions: Help your child to act out playing on park equipment.

The climber:
Up the rungs I go
As I climb so high.
Step up, step up, step up, step up,
Way up to the sky.

The swing:
The swing goes higher, higher still.
The wind blows right by me.
Now I swing so high I squeal.
Whee! Whee! Whee!

The seesaw:
Up and down, up and down,
I must hold so tight.
Up so high, now down so low,
This ride is a delight.

———

Dear Jesus,
Thank You for fun places. Amen.

To the adult: *Time on a playground brings a child close to "heaven on earth." A playground visit can be brief, but usually is a great experience. And the best might be yet to come: a young child usually sleeps very well after an outing at the park!*

Let us kneel before the Lord,
our Maker!   Psalm 95:6

Up and Down

Instructions: Encourage your child to go up and down as indicated.

Here I go up.
Here I go down.
What goes up?
   ♦ the barber's chair
   ♦ an elevator
   ♦ and me!

Here I go down.
Here I go up.
What goes down?
   ♦ a bouncing ball
   ♦ an elevator
   ♦ and me!

Here I go up.
Here I go down.
Here I go up and down.
Now I'll kneel and pray:

———————

Dear Jesus,
   Up and down I go each day. Thank You,
Lord, I now will pray. Amen.

To the adult: *Up and down are some of the first directional words a young child understands. "I'll pick you up" and "Now you lie down" are things we say often to an infant. Right and left are two of the last directional words a child comprehends. Your child will probably learn those, though, when the time is right. In the meantime, simply use all kinds of directional words whenever possible. You'll find that will help you give specific directions and will enrich your child's vocabulary and understanding.*

Sing to the Lord, all the world!
Psalm 100:1

A Joyful Noise

Instructions: Encourage your child to participate.

The writer in the Bible says, "Make a joyful
noise."
So listen as I shout "Hooray" like other girls
and boys.
Jesus is my Lord. I can jump up high.
Jesus is my Lord. I can reach the sky.
Jesus is my Lord. I can wiggle my nose.
Jesus is my Lord. I can tap my toes.
Jesus is my Lord. I can turn around.
Jesus is my Lord. I can touch the ground.
Praise the Lord!

Dear Jesus,
Thank You for all the things I can do. Amen.

To the adult: *Asking that your child grow up happy in the Lord is a prayer
of many parents. You are taking the time and making the effort to help that
happen. What a blessing you are to one of God's young children!*

My children, our love . . .
must be true love.   1 John 3:18

Listen to Me!

Instructions: Encourage your child to make the appropriate sounds.

I can make a sound like a car.
I can make a sound like a vacuum cleaner.
I can make a sound like a baby.
I can make a sound like a clock.
I can make a sound like a hammer.
I can sing a song to Jesus:
  (If your child hesitates, sing "Jesus
    Loves Me" with your child):
  "Jesus loves me, this I know
    For the Bible tells me so.
  Little ones to Him belong.
    They are weak but He is strong.
  Yes, Jesus loves me. Yes, Jesus loves me.
    Yes, Jesus loves me, the Bible tells me
so."

Dear Jesus,
  I like to sing to You. Amen.

To the adult: *Help your child make music with water glasses. Simply fill glass drinking glasses with various amounts of water: one can have just an inch of water, one can be full, etc. Your child can lightly tap each glass with a spoon, then listen to the different pitches. Sing "Jesus Loves Me" again, this time while your child taps the tune on the glasses. (As with any activity involving breakables, please carefully supervise your child during this activity.)*

I have called you by name—
you are mine.   Isaiah 43:1

A Rainbow Person

Instructions: Give your child a mirror to help her answer these questions.

What color eyes did God give you?
What color hair did God give you?
What color skin did God give you?
What color eyebrows did God give you?
(Now encourage your child to respond with the
    answers:)

God gave me _____ eyes.
God gave me _____ hair.
God gave me _____ skin.
God gave me _____ eyebrows.
God made me a rainbow person.

_____

Dear Jesus,
    Thank You for making me so color-full. Amen.

To the adult: *Do this activity again, having your child describe the colors God made you.*

I create both light and darkness.
Isaiah 45:7

Day and Night

Instructions: Encourage your child to act out these lines.

In the daytime the sun shines.
In the daytime the birds chirp.
In the daytime squirrels hop from tree to tree.
I run and jump and play.
And Jesus is with me.

The night comes.

In the nighttime the sun goes down.
In the nighttime the birds sleep.
In the nighttime the squirrels curl up.
I fall asleep in bed. And Jesus is with me.

Dear Jesus,
Thank You for always being with me. Amen.

To the adult: *Fear of the dark is common among young children. Encourage your child to talk about being afraid. When appropriate, talk about times when you were afraid. Children need to understand it's okay to be scared sometimes—and to be comforted by the fact that Jesus is always with them.*

Show me a man who does a good job.
Proverbs 22:29

Whoops!

Instructions: Encourage your child to act out the verses.

When a button falls off—whoops!
We need to sew.
In and out, in and out: sew the button.
Thanks, God, for people who sew buttons.

When a nail comes loose—whoops!
We need to hammer.
Tap, tap, tap, tap: hammer the nail.
Thanks, God, for people who hammer nails.

When a tire goes flat—whoops!
We need to pump.
Whoosh-air, whoosh-air, pump the tire.
Thanks, God, for people who fix tires.

Dear Jesus,
Thanks for people who do all sorts of jobs. Amen.

To the adult: *A child's circle of acquaintances gradually expands from family to friends to the neighborhood. Your child will first identify people by the uniforms they wear: nurse, letter carrier, store clerk, baseball player. A worn shirt can easily become a "uniform" for your child's playtime. For example: a white, adult-sized shirt with rolled up sleeves makes a great "uniform" for any junior-sized health worker.*

I made you and will care for you.
Isaiah 46:4

Fingers

Instructions: Encourage your child to use his fingers during this verse.

My fingers, I have ten of them,
Do so very much.
They pull, they rub, they tap and flop,
And now they even touch.
They point up high to God's blue sky
And to the ground below.
They snap, they bend, they wiggle,
And reach down to touch a toe.
My fingers can move back and forth
As trees sway in the breeze.
My fingers are so quiet
As I pray upon my knees:

Dear Jesus,
Thanks for hands that help me touch
and hug. Amen.

To the adult: *How many other groups of ten can your child count today? Begin with his fingers, toes, your fingers, strands of hair, etc.*

Do what your father tells you and
never forget what your mother
taught you.   Proverbs 6:20

Huggin' Time

Instructions: Hug your young child as appropriate.

Here's a special hug; it's meant for only you.
You're a favorite person; I love the things we do.

Here's a special hug, because I love you so,
Like Jesus loved his friends those many
      years ago.

Here's a special hug, because you are so dear.
And even when I can't be close,
      I know that God is near.

Here's a very special hug, because I'm filled
      with love
For you, the other dear ones, and Jesus from
      above.

Dear Jesus,
      Thanks for somebody who loves me. Amen.

To the adult: *As children grow up, we quite naturally spend less time cuddling them. But even that two-year-old, who sometimes isn't too lovable, needs hugs. Parents need hugs, too. Read this devotion again; this time your child can be the hugger and you can be the huggee!*

The trees in the woods will shout
for joy.   Psalm 96:12

Treehouses

Instructions: If possible, do this activity outdoors. Start off a short distance from a tree. Your child can run back and forth to the tree with each verse. Indoors, substitute any piece of furniture for the "tree."

"It's my house," says the bird. Flap, flap, flap
to the tree. God made trees for birds.

"It's my house," says the squirrel. Scamper,
scamper, scamper to the tree. God made
trees for squirrels.

"It's my house," says the ant. Walk, walk, walk
to the tree. God made trees for ants.

"It's my playhouse," says the child. Run, run,
run to the tree. God made trees for me!

Dear Jesus,
Thanks for trees. Amen.

To the adult: *Fall housecleaning can uncover wonderful raw materials for children to use in sorting, dressing up, and creating works of art. Save bits of trim, socks with holes, empty thread spools, and leftover paper towel tubes. Throw everything in a "not junk box." As long as there's nothing sharp, your child will enjoy the "treasure box" on some long winter day.*

It is good to be able to enjoy the pleasant light of day.
Ecclesiastes 11:7

Watch Me!

Instructions: Encourage your child to do this activity.

1.
Watch me.
I can twirl around one time.

1–2.
Watch me.
I can jump two times.

1–2–3.
Watch me.
I can hop on one foot three times.

1–2–3–4.
Watch me.
I can hop on the other foot four times.

1–2–3–4–5.
Watch me.
I can give you five kisses!

———————————————

Dear Jesus,
Thanks for Your fun times. Amen.

To the adult: *Did you and your child laugh together today? So much of parenting is hard work, it's tempting to forget to have fun. Take time out for fun—with activities like these—the next time you feel grumpy.*

Go up on a high mountain and
proclaim the good news!

Isaiah 40:9

Mountains and Plains

Instructions: In this action verse, your child can wave hands up in the air for the "mountains" and down near the ground for the "plains."

God put trees
High in the mountains,
Down on the plains.

God put animals
High in the mountains,
Down on the plains.

God put birds
High in the mountains,
Down on the plains.

God put flowers
High in the mountains,
Down on the plains.

God put me right here!

Dear Jesus,
   I'm glad You put me here. Amen.

To the adult: *Read this verse slowly the first time, then speed up the pace each time you repeat. This activity easily bridges the gap between older and younger children, especially as the pace increases.*

*Then He got up and ordered the winds
and the waves to stop, and there was a
great calm.*   Matthew 8:26

The Storm

Instructions: Give your child two pan lids to bang together to provide the
sound effects as indicated for this story.

In a small boat,
On a big lake,
Went Jesus and His friends.

A storm came up (*bang, bang*).
The sky grew dark (*bang, bang*)
Over Jesus and His friends.

The lightning cracked (*bang, bang*).
The thunder crashed (*bang, bang*)
Around Jesus and His friends.

"Wake up, wake up" (*bang, bang*),
The people said (*bang, bang*).
"Wake, Jesus!" called His friends.

Jesus woke up
And said, "Be still."
The storm was done
For Jesus and His friends.

Dear Jesus,
Storms can be scary. I'm glad You helped
Your friends. Amen.

To the adult: *Your child can reenact this story in the bathroom sink. Shape
aluminum foil into a "boat." (For a fancy mast stick a toothpick into play
dough or into a prune.) Read the story again, without the "bang, bang."*

O Lord, my God, how great You are!
                    Psalm 104:1

Climb Up

Instructions: As you read this verse, encourage your child to slowly walk her fingers from one hand up the other arm. At the end she should be near her face.

A hill.
A hill of sand.
A hill of sand on the sidewalk.

Climb up.
Climb up to the top.
Climb up to the top of the anthill.

God watches.
God watches over His creatures.
God watches over His creatures and me.

Dear Jesus,
    I know You watch over little things like ants.
    I'm glad You watch over big people like me.
    Amen.

To the adult: *Ants are child-sized creatures that build child-sized places to live. Your child will enjoy playing with a stick and a crawling ant. Show her how to be gentle with God's creatures.*

I will sing You a new song, O God.
Psalm 144:9

Singing Fun

Instructions: Sing this verse to the tune, "Twinkle, Twinkle, Little Star."

I can clap my hands up high.
Watch me clap them in the sky.
Take my hands and clap, clap, clap.
Now my feet go tap, tap, tap.
I am Jesus' child I know,
For the Bible tells me so.

I can walk on my tip-toes.
Then reach up and touch my nose.
Take my fingers tap, tap, tap.
Make my feet go stamp, stamp, stamp.
I am Jesus' little one.
Jesus loves me, God's dear Son.

God gives me so many parts:
Hands and shoulders, feet and heart.
For it's with my heart I love
Jesus, Son of God, above.
He alone created me
And He guides me happily.

———————

Dear Jesus,
 I like to sing about You. Amen.

To the adult: *Learning about his body—and what it can do—is a major part of life for a young child. He's probably learning about snaps and buttons and zippers too. Tying a shoelace, though, is a complicated activity that he'll learn much later. Always encourage, never push.*

Give thanks to the Lord, proclaim
His greatness.   Psalm 105:1

Sit a Spell

Instructions: Pull a chair—preferably child-sized—into the center of the room for your child to sit on during this devotion. Also encourage her to act out the different activities.

I can sit on a bike and pedal fast.
I can sit in the car, "Please step on the gas."
I can sit on a park bench and watch the kites fly.

I can sit in an airplane, see houses go by.
I can sit in a church to pray and sing.
That's where I thank God for everything.

———————————

Dear Jesus,
    Thanks for places to go and things to see. Amen.

To the adult: *Your child can easily set up the seats for an "airplane" or "car." Line up chairs in pairs. Cut a 2" strip from a paper bag and lay it on each chair for a seat belt.*

The land has produced its harvest.
Psalm 67:6

It All Falls Down

Instructions: Encourage your child to act out these lines.

The leaves fall: swish, swish.
The acorns fall: kerplop, kerplop.
The raindrops fall: drip, drip.
The pinecones fall: plop, plop.

Many things fall in autumn.
Soon God will send something else to fall.
The snow will fall: softly, softly.
Have a good winter's nap, earth.

Dear Jesus,
  My favorite thing about autumn is ⎯⎯⎯⎯ .
Amen.

To the adult: *Now is the time to plan for that first really cold day. Your young child has probably grown a lot since last year. Keep handy one warm outfit for your child, so outside play is possible even if temperatures drop suddenly.*

As I lie in bed, I remember You.
Psalm 63:6

Good Night

Instructions: This is an ideal poem to use at bedtime.

When the sky is dark and the sun goes down,
It's nighttime. It's not light-time.
Good night sun.

When the sky is dark and the moon comes up,
It's nighttime. It's not light-time.
Good night, moon.

When the sky is dark and the stars come out,
It's nighttime. It's not light-time.
Good night, stars.

When the sky is dark,
The sun goes down,
The moon comes up,
The stars come out.
It's nighttime.
It's not light-time.
It's my bedtime.
Good night, God.

Dear Jesus,
  Thank You for the stars so bright and moon
  that lightens up the night. Amen.

To the adult: *As a child, did you have a favorite bedtime song or lullaby?*
Ask family members and relatives to help you tape "family-favorite" lullabies.
Even your very young child will then fall asleep listening to a family tradition.

The Lord will guard you; He is by
your side to protect you. Psalm 121:5

My Friend, Jesus

Instructions: Walk through this activity with your child.

I can walk all alone.
I can walk with a friend.
Jesus walks with me.

I can walk very fast.
I can walk very slow.
Jesus is with me.

I can walk with tiny steps.
I can walk with giant steps.
Jesus is with me.

Dear Jesus,
Thanks for being with me. Amen.

To the adult: *How does your child view Jesus? Young children often develop "imaginary friends." Some young children even see Jesus in this way. Developmentally, we know that is appropriate. What is so wonderful about sharing the Christian faith with a child is that soon the child will understand that Jesus is real, and offers so much more than an imaginary friend.*

Whoever believes that Jesus is the Messiah is a child of God. 1 John 5:1

I Can

Instructions: Ask your child to nod "yes" to everything he can do.

I can sneeze.
I can crawl.
I can stamp my feet.
I can whisper.
I can cough.
I can shake hands.
I can say a prayer to Jesus:

———————————

Dear Jesus,
Thank You for helping me grow up. Amen.

To the adult: *Emphasize the "can dos." That's important when working with young children—there are simply so many things they can't accomplish yet. Being positive, beginning activities with a smile, and saying "You did a good job" are very important in positive parenting. But the "can dos" need to be emphasized by parents. You are, right now, doing one of the most important actions any parent can do: helping a young child grow with Jesus. That's a "can do" that lasts a lifetime, and beyond.*

I was glad when they said to me,
"Let us go to the Lord's house."
Psalm 122:1

Building Blocks

Instructions: Encourage your child to count 1–2–3.

Let's build a church now:
1–2–3.
Let's build it high
For you and me.
Let's walk inside now:
1–2–3.
Let's pray to Jesus
Just you and me.

Dear Jesus,
I like to go to church. Amen.

To the adult: *Does your child build "houses" that don't look like houses? Or does your toddler "play blocks" by simply carrying around a block? There are distinct developmental stages to block building. Your child will progress from simply holding a block to creating complicated structures which represent something in "real life." Children go through the same stages, but spend varying amounts of time at each stage.*

What a rich harvest Your goodness
provides! Psalm 65:11

What's Cooking?

Instructions: You and your child can clap once on each syllable of this verse.

This good food tastes airy.
This good food has bumps.
This good food sounds crunchy.
This good food looks white.
This good food even smells good.
This good food is popcorn!

―――――――――――

Dear Jesus,
 Thanks for fun food like popcorn. Amen.

To the adult: *You and your child can have fun "popping popcorn." Take an old crib or twin sheet. You might even cut a hole in the center to make it a parachute. You and your child can hold opposite sides of the sheet. Then raise and lower the sheet while you "pop corn." White ping pong balls make ideal "corn" to bounce up and down, but a child's shoe also works fine. This is great fun when you need a break from routine.*

The hillsides are full of joy.

Psalm 65:12

Autumn Song

Instructions: Encourage your child to act out these words while you sing to the tune of "Frère Jacques" (Are You Sleeping).

Leaves are falling,
Leaves are falling,
All around, all around.
Red and yellow twirling.
God sends winds to swirl them
To the ground,
To the ground.

Pinecones falling,
Pinecones falling,
All around, all around.
Cracking as they tumble.
Breaking as they crumble
On the ground,
On the ground.

Dear Jesus,
    I know fall is when the earth gets ready to
    take a nap. Amen.

To the adult: *With your help, your child can make a leaf rubbing. Peel a crayon. Lay a thin piece of paper over a leaf your child has found. Your child can rub the crayon on the paper which covers the leaf.*

Don't let anything worry you.
Ecclesiastes 11:10

Scary Times

Instructions: Your child can clap hands at every word-sound.

When a balloon goes *pop*,
Sometimes I get scared.

When thunder goes *clap*,
Sometimes I get scared.

When something falls with a *boom*,
Sometimes I get scared.

When a clown says *boo*,
Sometimes I get scared.

When a firecracker goes *bang*,
Sometimes I get scared.

That's when I pray:

———————————

Dear Jesus,
Be with me. Amen.

To the adult: *Some of your young child's fears are easy to understand: fear of the dark, storms, big dogs. But other fears might seem irrational: the fear of balloons, for example, or candles on a birthday cake. Some children go to extraordinary lengths (such as hiding under a table at a birthday party!) to get away from such things. Young children might go through many stages with various fears. During these times, provide support, quiet assurance, and know that the fear will probably dissolve within the next year or so.*

God has blessed us.
Psalm 67:7

Cornstalks

Instructions: Encourage your child to use her hands in this fingerplay.

Five cornstalks standing straight and tall.
Five cornstalks standing; soon they'll fall.
The farmer will cut them down.
1–2–3–4–5 touch the ground.
This harvest time brings special cheer.
Pop, pop, pop is what I hear!

Dear Jesus,
Thanks for popcorn. Amen.

To the adult: *Warnings from the medical community encourage adults to carefully supervise children under 3 when they eat foods such as popcorn and peanuts.*

How good it is to give thanks to You,
O Lord. Psalm 92:1

Brown Signs

Instructions: Look outside for this activity.

There are many signs of fall. See if you can
guess these riddles:

♦ It is brown. It fell from a tree. I rake it up.
It is a _____ (leaf).

♦ It is brown. It scampers around. It looks for
nuts to bury. It has a bushy tail.
It is a _____ (squirrel).

♦ It is brown now. It was green in summer. It
grew so long, we cut it with a lawn mower.
It is _____ (grass).

—————————————

Dear Jesus,
It's autumn. You're with me. Thanks. Amen.

To the adult: *Your child might want to carry a sand pail along on your next*
walk. Help him collect things from nature that are brown.

Sounds for Jesus

Instructions: Encourage your child to make the appropriate sounds.

A little train said, "Toot toot."
I can "toot" for Jesus.
Toot-toot-toot. Praise God!

A little cement mixer said, "Rumble, rumble."
I can "rumble" for Jesus.
Rumble-rumble-rumble. Praise God!

A little fire engine said, "Whirr, whirr."
I can "whirr" for Jesus.
Whirr-whirr-whirr. Praise God!

A little boat said, "Putt, putt."
I can "putt" for Jesus.
Putt-putt-putt. Praise God!

A little child said, "I can make all those noises.
I can toot-toot.
I can rumble-rumble.
I can whirr-whirr.
I can putt, putt.
I can praise God.
I can also tell Jesus I love Him."

———————————

Dear Jesus,
    I love You. Amen.

To the adult: *How many sounds can your child make using an empty toilet paper roll?*

Let the children come to Me and do not
stop them. Matthew 19:14

"Come to Me"

Instructions: Encourage your child to count on her fingers as appropriate.

Once Jesus called some little ones,
"Come here and sit near me.
I want to see each one of you,
So come now, 1–2–3."

The children came to Jesus fast;
They sat upon His knee.
1–2–3–4–5–6–7–8
"I'm glad you came to me."

Now Jesus calls us—you and me—
Today and every day.
1–2–3–4–5–6–7–8
He'd like to hear us pray:

———————————

Dear Jesus,
    I'm glad I'm important to You. Amen.

To the adult: *Can your child act out this Bible story with stuffed animals and toys?*

God looked at everything He had made,
and He was very pleased.
                              Genesis 1:31

Leaf Turnover

Instructions: Do this activity outside with your child, or bring a few leaves indoors.

Turn over a leaf.
What do I see?
Highways for plantfood and water.

Turn over a leaf.
What do I see?
Some colors of God's rainbow.

Turn over a leaf.
What do I see?
Some humps and bumps that I can feel.

———————————

Dear Jesus,
     Thank You for autumn. Amen.

To the adult: *Make it easy for your young child to learn independence doing autumn clean-up chores. A child can handle a small-sized rake, but the child will also need a place to store the rake. Children can put away sandbox toys for the winter, but storage must be low to the ground. Build in ways, right now, that help a young child be independent.*

Come and see what the Lord has done.
Psalm 46:8

Animals in Autumn

Instructions: Encourage your child to act out this verse.

The squirrels scamper here and there
with nuts to bury deep.
They'll gobble up those nuts for snacks
when they wake up from sleep.
The snakes squirm in the forest
with their tummies on the ground.
They slither to a hiding place
so they will not be found.
The birds fly south across the sky,
wings flapping as they go.
They are in such a hurry now
not even one is slow.
Why do God's woodland creatures all
now slither, scamper, fly?
They know the winter's coming so
to fall they say "Good-bye."

———————————

Dear Jesus,
Thank You for telling the animals how to get
ready for winter. Amen.

To the adult: *On the next walk with your child, talk about how God's world is protected during the winter: bark is a "coat" for a tree; leaves provide a "blanket" for the ground; animals—even the family dog—might grow a thicker coat, etc.*

It is love, then, that you should
strive for.   1 Corinthians 14:1

Tap a Tune

Instructions: Your child can tap a spoon on the table on every word of this echo verse. You will say a line; your child will repeat it, tapping.

I love Jesus. (*I love Jesus.*)
You love Jesus. (*You love Jesus.*)
We love Jesus. (*We love Jesus.*)
I tell others. (*I tell others.*)
You tell others. (*You tell others.*)
We tell others. (*We tell others.*)
I'm His helper. (*I'm His helper.*)
You're His helper. (*You're His helper.*)
We're His helpers. (*We're His helpers.*)

———————

Dear Jesus,
    I like telling people about You. Amen.

To the adult: *Children are natural music-makers when it comes to rhythm. They will have fun clapping the rhythm of the names of those who love them: Jesus, mommy, grandpa, sister, etc.*

Praise Him for the mighty things
He has done.   Psalm 150:2

Ten

Instructions: Encourage your child to count as indicated.

I remember when it was winter.
I counted all my fingers in my gloves.
1-2-3-4-5-6-7-8-9-10

I remember when it was spring.
I counted 10 raindrops in the puddle.
1-2-3-4-5-6-7-8-9-10

I remember when it was summer.
I counted my toes wiggling in the pool.
1-2-3-4-5-6-7-8-9-10

Now it is autumn.
I can count 10 leaves on the ground.
1-2-3-4-5-6-7-8-9-10

Dear Jesus,
    Thanks for all the times of year. Amen.

To the adult: *Some events in our lives as parents will be etched forever in our memories. But much of our time as parents simply floats by. Photographs can help us "remember when." Consider taking a picture of your child next to a small tree or shrub on the first day of each new season. Date your photo. Years from now you will look back on those photos and "remember when." Some parents like to take this idea a bit further and plant a tree on a child's birthday, and then use that child's tree in the photos. "Me and my tree" then becomes a great memory book for the child and parent.*

The Lord takes pleasure in His people.
Psalm 149:4

Listen!

Instructions: Encourage your child to make the appropriate sounds.

God gave me ears
so I can hear:
- ♦ a motorcycle roar—rrrrrr
- ♦ an ambulance siren—whooooooo
- ♦ a church bell—ding dong
- ♦ a train whistle—choo! choo!

"Happy Thanksgiving!"

Dear Jesus,
Help me remember to say "thank you"
for all You give. Amen.

To the adult: *Many parents keep baby books and picture records. But a sound recording of our child's development can bring back the happiest of memories years from now. As you talk with your baby, and listen to your toddler, turn on a tape to record those sounds. A finished product isn't important—just capture the sounds and note the date. There will be time in the future to "edit it" if you choose.*

I am the God who forgives your sins.
Isaiah 43:25

Let's Build

Instructions: Get a stack of building blocks or anything small that can be piled high for a tower: spools of thread, plastic containers, books, etc. Add to your steeple as indicated by the numerals.

Let's build a steeple 1–2–3.
Let's build a steeple, just you and me.
Let's build a steeple, 4–5–6.

Let's build a steeple made of bricks.
Let's build a steeple 7–8–9.
Let's build a steeple. Will it be fine?
(It falls.) The steeple fell down.

———

Dear Jesus,
Sometimes it happens: things don't work right.
But Jesus forgives me and says, "It's all right."
Amen.

To the adult: *We practice forgiveness each day. As adults, we need to give children the assurance of our forgiveness and Christ's forgiveness. But we also need to remember that when we're not the parent we want to be or hope to be, God forgives us, too. He gives us the chance to try again.*

When He spoke, the world was created.
Psalm 33:9

A Pet

Instructions: Encourage your child to act out the various lines.

A pet might swim in a bowl.
A pet might dig a big hole.
A pet might sit in your lap.
A pet would be good for that!

A pet might chirp tweet, tweet, tweet.
A pet might kiss you so sweet.
A pet might woof bow, wow, wow.
A pet might whisper me-ow.

Dear Jesus,
Thank You for creating pets. Amen.

To the adult: *Children and pets go together. That's often true in artists' illustrations and sometimes true in life. For a young child, the best pet might be one the child visits at grandma's or a neighbor's.*

Your praise . . . is sung by children.
Psalm 8:2

Fall Is Here

Instructions: Encourage your child to act out the verses as you sing to the tune of "Here We Go 'Round the Mulberry Bush."

Watch me as I rake the leaves,
Rake the leaves, rake the leaves.
Watch me as I rake the leaves,
For God says fall is here.

Watch me as I bake a pie,
Bake a pie, bake a pie.
Watch me as I bake a pie,
From a big fat pumpkin.

Watch me as I put away,
Put away, put away.
Watch me as I put away,
All my summer toys.

———————————

Dear Jesus,
Autumn is here and I feel —————— . Amen.

To the adult: *Make up your own verses. For example: Put away summer clothes, take a nice long nap, etc.*

He supplies the needs of those who
honor Him. Psalm 145:19

Kitchen Fun

Instructions: Encourage your child to act out this verse.

Sifting, sifting. We'll bake a pie.
Whoops! Don't touch.
The pan is hot.
Thank You, God, for food.

Stirring, stirring. Let's make some gravy.
Whoops! Don't touch.
The pot is hot.
Thank You, God, for food.

Kneading, kneading. We'll bake some bread.
Whoops! Don't touch.
The bread will rise.
Thank You, God, for food.

Sniffing, sniffing. My nose is working.
Great! Let's eat.
God gives us food.
Thank You, God, for food.

Dear Jesus,
My favorite Thanksgiving Day food is _____ .
Amen.

To the adult: *Even a young child can help make finger gelatin. Dissolve four small packages of any flavor gelatin in 2½ cups boiling water in a bowl. Stir to dissolve. Pour into 8 or 9″ square pan. Chill at least four hours. Cut into holiday shapes with cookie cutters. The scraps taste great, too!*

Come and see what God has done.
Psalm 66:5

Finger Fun

Instructions: Encourage your child to use fingers for this playtime.

These are my ten fingers;
God gave them all to me.
These are my two thumbs;
I wiggle them now, see?
My little pinkies are so small
That I just let them be.
And then that leaves the other ones;
I count them 1, 2, 3.
These are my ten fingers;
God gave them all to me.

––––––––––––––––

Dear Jesus,
I pray when my fingers go together.
Thank You, Jesus. Amen.

To the adult: *Young children delight in seeing how their fingers can help make a "hand turkey." Spread out your child's hand on a piece of paper. Trace around each of the fingers, up to the wrist. A turkey will appear!*

I will give You thanks forever.
Psalm 30:12

The Garage

Instructions: Encourage your child to learn how the various tools are used.

What's in a garage?

♦ A rake gathers the leaves.
Leaves fall from the trees.
Rake-rake-rake.

♦ A shovel moves the snow
when the cold winds blow.
Shovel-shovel-shovel.

♦ A hoe digs the ground
when weeds are around.
dig-dig-dig.

♦ A car? Oh, yes.
A car has a place in the leftover space!
Vroom-vroom.

Dear Jesus,
Thanks for things and places to keep them. Amen.

To the adult: *How do you store all those bulky child-related "essentials"? A clearly marked storage area (garage, hallway, etc.) will help you. A "parking lot" will also help your young child develop good habits of putting away. In the garage, for example, use chalk or masking tape on the floor to mark places for the stroller and tricycle. You and your child can find pictures of similar items in a catalog. Cut out the pictures and paste them on paper. Hang the paper on the wall in the appropriate "parking space." Your child will find it great fun to be "parking lot supervisor."*

[God] changes rocks into pools of water.
Psalm 114:8

Water

Instructions: Encourage your child to show the ways he uses water.

I can wash my face.
Splash, splash, splash.
I can water the flowers.
Drink, drink, drink.
I can clean my toys.
Scrub, scrub, scrub.
I can hold an umbrella.
Drip, drip, drop.

Dear Jesus,
Water feels wet. I like water when _____ .
Amen.

To the adult: *Collect a group of bathtub toys that float: styrofoam cups, bits of aluminum foil, plastic silverware. Your child might enjoy a "pretend" floating meal on a thin plastic placemat!*

"Let's go to Bethlehem."
Luke 2:15

What Happened?

Instructions: Encourage your child to make the appropriate sounds.

When Jesus was born
a cow might have mooed.
When Jesus was born
a dove might have cooed.
When Jesus was born
a donkey might have brayed.
When Jesus was born
a horse might have neighed.
Now Jesus was born
and I can say:
"Jesus of Bethlehem,
Happy Birthday."

Dear Jesus,
Christmas is coming. I'm glad. Amen.

To the adult: *Your child can easily make napkin rings to use for holiday meals. Simply cut off a 1-inch strip from an empty toilet paper roll. Your child can decorate with Christmas stickers.*

The water . . . was a symbol pointing
to baptism.   1 Peter 3:20–21

Tickle My Back!

Instructions: For this activity, have your child sit with her back facing you. Using your fingers trace different Christmas symbols on your child's back. Can your child guess what you're drawing? Use the extra clues if your child needs help.

Heart (reminds us Jesus loves us)
Candle (something we put on Jesus' birthday cake)

Star (what the Wise Men looked at in the sky)
Cross (Jesus died for us)

———————————

Dear Jesus,
    I liked this tickly game. Thanks for fun times, like Your birthday. Amen.

To the adult: *As the busy days of December tick away, use this game again with variations. Trace the first letter of your child's name, Jesus' name, etc. Playing "tickle my back" will give you and your child quality moments during this busy season—and a great excuse to sit down and rest!*

Glory to God in the highest heaven.
Luke 2:14

C-H-R-I-S-T-M-A-S-Y

Instructions: Encourage your child to use his ten fingers for this fingerplay.

C is for Christmas, Jesus' birthday.
H is for happy, and that's for me.
R is for robe, that kept Jesus warm.
I is for innkeeper who lent a room free.
S is for star, high in the sky.
T is for three (Wisemen), who rode through the
     night.
M is for Mary, mother of the babe.
A is for angels, who looked so bright.
S is for shepherds who came right away.
Y is for you! Happy Jesus' birthday.

Dear Jesus,
     I used my fingers, all of them, to tell Your birthday
     story again. Amen.

To the adult: *Even young children are introduced to the Santa vs. Jesus struggle. When a child focuses on simple fingerplays like this, and enjoys a happy celebration of Jesus' birth, no one even thinks of Santa!*

Jesus was born in the town of Bethlehem.
Matthew 2:1

Christmas Fun

Instructions: Encourage your child to act out this verse.

I would laugh
if the shepherd's staff
were a candy cane.
I would bite
a star cookie in the night
but the Magi's star was real.
I like to eat
all kinds of Christmas treats
that remind me of Jesus.
But all the while,
as I smile, I'm most happy that Jesus was born
for me.

Dear Jesus,
Thank You for the fun times of Christmas. Amen.

To the adult: *With the pressures of holiday activities, it's easy to lose sight of the true joy of Christmas. That's one thing that makes Christmas with a young child such fun: they laugh, smile, and really enjoy. What a privilege to share a first, or second, or third Christmas with a child. As you experience the real joy of Christ's birth, may you have a most blessed Christmastide.*

I am here with good news for you.
Luke 2:10

Counting Up Christmas

Instructions: Help your child with this fingerplay. Begin with the little finger.

Here's the mother of Jesus (little finger)
and Joseph stands so tall (ring finger)
Now two shepherds from the field,
do we have them all?
We're missing Baby Jesus (thumb)
born on Christmas Day.
Happy birthday, Jesus,
is what we have to say.

Dear Jesus,
Happy Birthday. Amen.

To the adult: *This fingerplay offers an easy way for a child to focus on the real meaning of Christmas. Your child might want to learn this for sharing with friends and relatives during the holidays.*

They told them what the angel had said
about the Child.   Luke 2:17

Bake a Birthday Cake

Instructions: Encourage your child to act out this song while you sing the following words to the tune of "Here We Go 'Round the Mulberry Bush."

This is the way I mix a cake,
mix a cake, mix a cake.
This is the way I mix a cake,
a birthday cake for Jesus.

This is the way I cut a cake,
cut a cake, cut a cake.
This is the way I cut a cake,
a birthday cake for Jesus.

This is the way I eat a cake,
eat a cake, eat a cake.
This is the way I eat a cake,
a birthday cake for Jesus.

Dear Jesus,
I love You. Amen.

To the adult: *Children can easily identify with the idea of Jesus' birthday. Some families settle the "mince or pumpkin pie" dispute by serving a Jesus birthday cake for the holiday dessert. How many candles will be on your Jesus birthday cake? Your young child will love putting on the candles and even arranging a small crèche set on the frosted cake.*

This very day in David's town your
Savior was born—Christ the Lord!
Luke 2:11

Ring, Ring

Instructions: For this activity, tie jingle bells onto your child's shoelaces, or give her a bell to ring—even a Christmas ornament bell will work well.

> I can sing. I can sing.
> Jesus is born.
> I can shout. I stamp about.
> Jesus is born.
> I can clap. I can tap.
> Jesus is born.
> I can tell, ring my bell.
> Jesus is born.

> Dear Jesus,
> My song today is "It's Your Birthday." Amen.

To the adult: *Keep a tape recorder handy today. Start recording as you and your child sing Christmas carols. Try to tape your child's "telling" of the Christmas story, if appropriate. Date your tape, whether or not it sounds professional. After the holidays, pack it away with the crèche set. Next year, start recording as your child helps you unpack the manger figures. The informal chatter of your own Christmas child will be a precious keepsake years from now.*

Blink, Blink

Instructions: Give your child a flashlight for this devotion. Your child can blink the flashlight on every time you read, "Jesus, the Light of the world."

It's Christmas.
Jesus is born for me.
Jesus the Light of the world.

It's Christmas.
Jesus was born in Bethlehem.
Jesus the Light of the world.

It's Christmas.
Jesus is my Savior.
Jesus the Light of the world.

It's Christmas.
Happy birthday, Jesus.
Jesus the Light of the world.

Dear Jesus,
      Happy Birthday. Amen.

To the adult: *A flashlight and batteries is a wonderful Christmas gift for a child. Take a flashlight along to the Christmas candlelight service, if you wish. For a young child, the artificial light makes a good substitute for a candle dripping hot wax.*

The time came for her to have
her baby.   Luke 2:6

What Do I Need for Christmas?

Instructions: Encourage your child to act out this verse.

What do I need for Christmas?
I need a tall, tall tree.
It must reach higher than I can.
Much higher up than me.

What do I need for Christmas?
I need a bell to ring.
"Ding dong, ding dong, ding"
Is what my bell will sing.

What do I need for Christmas?
I need a birthday time:
Jesus' happy birthday
Will make my Christmas fine.

Dear Jesus,
    Thank You for being born. Amen.

To the adult: *With the commercialization of Christmas, it's easy for a young child to miss the real meaning of Christ's birth. Some families put Christ in the center of their Christmas by adding one figure to the crèche set each day. Mary, Joseph, and animals are set out, one each day, on the days before Christmas, Jesus on Christmas, and the shepherds and Magi after Christmas.*

You will find a Baby wrapped in cloths.   Luke 2:12

Wrap It Up

Instructions: Encourage your child to act out this verse.

When I wrap a Christmas present,
I cut some pretty paper.
I cover the box.
I tape the paper.
I tie a bow.
It's all done.

When God sent His present to us,
Mary wrapped God's Gift with care.
She folded the cloth round and round,
And laid the Baby gently in a manger.
God sent the first Christmas present to us:
Baby Jesus.

Dear Jesus,
I'm glad You were born. Amen.

To the adult: *Large packages will be the easiest for your young child to wrap. Little gifts require too much fine motor control for most young children. If you involve your child in wrapping gifts—and that's a great idea—begin with an even surface, plan to hold the tape, and bring plenty of patience.*

[The star] went ahead of them.
Matthew 2:9–10

A Camel Ride

Instructions: For this devotion, cut out a crown from a brown paper bag for your child to wear. It's also ideal if your child can ride "camel back" while the two of you act out this verse.

Please hop on a camel
  and go find Jesus.
Just watch for a big star
  and you'll find Jesus.
Ride, ride, the camel now
  to search for Jesus.
Stop! Ask people you meet,
  "Have you seen Jesus?"
Ride, ride the camel now
  to search for Jesus.
Follow the shining star.
  We're getting closer.
It stopped! The star stopped here.
  Where is the baby?
Get off the camel now.
  Where is the baby?
There's the star, over there.
  Where is the baby? (Walk toward your
  own crèche.)
Here is baby Jesus.
  We have found Jesus.

Dear Jesus,
  I'm glad You were born. Amen.

To the adult: *Your child can decorate his crown by gluing on scraps of gift wrap paper.*

*I remember the days gone by; I think
about all that You have done.*
Psalm 143:5

Good-Bye and Hello

Instructions: Encourage your child to act out these lines.

> I can wave good-bye.
> I can give a good-bye hug.
> I can smile good-bye.
> I can give a good-bye kiss.
> Good-bye, old year.
>
> I can wave hello.
> I can give a hello hug.
> I can smile hello.
> I can give a hello kiss.
> Hello, new year.

> Dear Jesus,
> I end the old year with You. I will start the
> new year with You. Amen.

To the adult: *You might be one of the few people at your home celebrating the gift of a new year. This is because a young child's new year begins and ends on her birthday. So—have a blessed new year!*

Devotions for Special Days:

Topics of Special Interest for Adults:

Angels: 152
Art ideas: 58, 80, 94, 100, 112, 114, 120, 142,
   240, 270, 276, 296
Bedtime: 36, 52
Birthday: 22
Church: 108, 134, 164, 182
Encouragement: 50, 24, 132, 200, 212, 216, 234,
   262, 292
Fears:
   dogs: 76
   farm animals: 170
   carnival: 180
   dark: 206
   "unimportant": 242
Fingerplays: 68, 18, 210, 222, 244, 258, 270, 284
Food ideas: 30, 10, 126, 184, 268
Memory-making: 12, 230, 258, 260, 288
Moving: 88
Prayer: 18, 60
Vacation: 168
Waterplay: 34, 274

STORY
JOHNNY ZITO
TONY TROV
CHRISTIAN WIESER

LETTERS
GABE BAUTISTA

ART
PAUL MAYBURY

BOOK DESIGN
PAUL MAYBURY
JORDAN GIBSON

DOGS OF MARS
ISBN: 978-1-60706-550-0
May 2012. First Printing. Published by Image Comics, Inc. Office of publication: 2134 Allston Way, 2nd Floor, Berkeley, CA 94704.
Originally published in single magazine form as DOGS OF MARS #1-4. Copyright © 2012 Johnny Zito, Tony Trov and Christian
Wieser. All rights reserved. DOGS OF MARS™ (including all prominent characters featured herein), its logo and all character
likenesses are trademarks of Johnny Zito, Tony Trov and Christian Wieser, unless otherwise noted. Image Comics® and its logos
are registered trademarks of Image Comics, Inc. No part of this publication may be reproduced or transmitted, in any form or by
any means (except for short excerpts for review purposes) without the express written permission of Image Comics, Inc. All names,
characters, events and locales in this publication are entirely fictional. Any resemblance to actual persons (living or dead), events
or places, without satiric intent, is coincidental. PRINTED IN KOREA.

International Rights Representative: Christine Meyer (christine@gfloystudio.com).

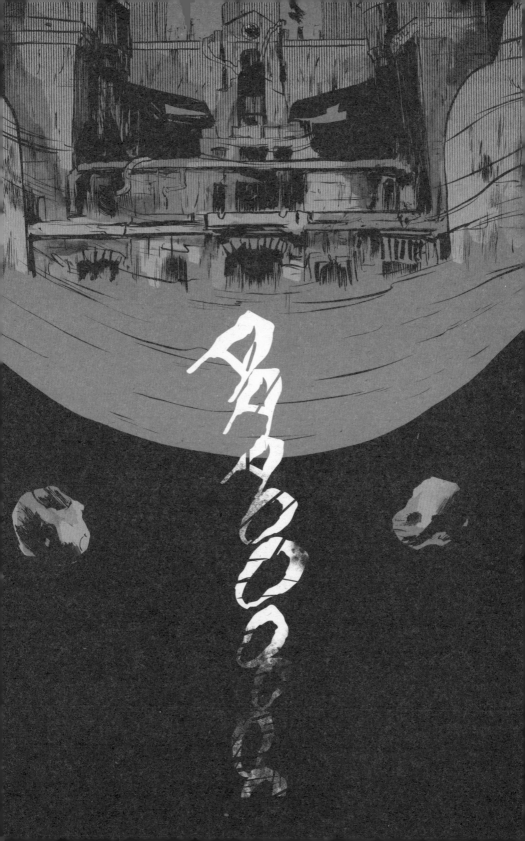

KEEP DREAMING ZOE!

GET 'EM!

WE GOT DESSERT RATIONS ON YOU, DOC!

HEY, TURK, YOU WANT A BEER?

HM? OH. NO THANKS, ISHMAEL

IT'S ISAIAH ACTUALLY.

BETTER LUCK NEXT TIME.

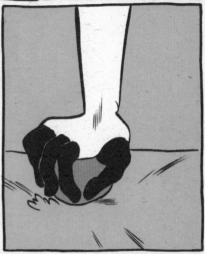

SO FAR WE'VE BEEN CHEMICALLY TREATING THE SURFACE BUT PHASE TWO IS WHERE THINGS GET REALLY COOL.

INTRODUCING; STAR MAN; THE MOST POWERFUL ATOMIC BOMB EVER BUILT.

AND WE'RE GONNA DROP IT RIGHT INTO THE CENTER OF MARS.

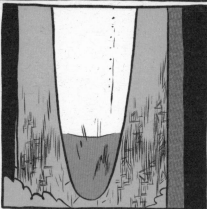

THAT SHOULD KICK START THE PLANET'S MOLTEN CORE—

AND SPONTANEOUSLY GENERATE A MAGNETIC FIELD AROUND THE PLANET.

KA-BOOM!

MR. KHAN, YOU APPEAR TO HAVE BROKEN EVERYTHING.

ROVER LOST THE WIRELESS SIGNAL....SOME KIND OF INTERFERENCE.

FINALLY! PEACE AND QUIET.

POWER FAILURE IS STATIONWIDE. *GULP* WE CAN'T CONNECT WITH THE GENERATORS.

MUST BE A STORM COMING.

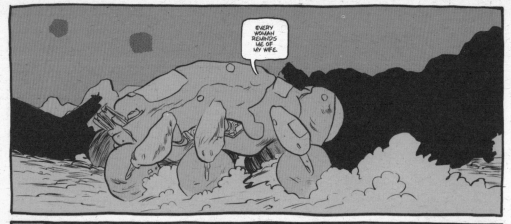

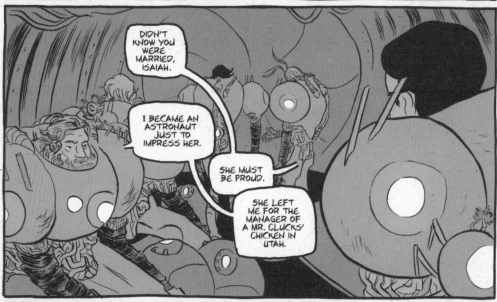

THE TWO FULL MOONS ARE GIVING OFF ODD GRAVITY SIGNATURES THAT ARE SCREWING WITH WIRELESS POWER AND COMMUNICATIONS.

THE LUNAR EVENT LASTS FOR 26 HOURS AND HAPPENS ONLY ONCE EVERY 30 YEARS.

WE SHOULD WAIT FOR DAYLIGHT.

DON'T WORRY ALL THE TIME; YOU'LL WRINKLE.

SCARED OF THE DARK?

I'M JUST SAYING, IF I WERE IN CHARGE, WE'D DO IT DIFFERENTLY.

THE GOOD OLD DAYS.

IN THE OLD DAYS, YOU COULD JUST SHOOT ME IN THE BACK AND STEAL MY HORSE.

KRRSSH!!

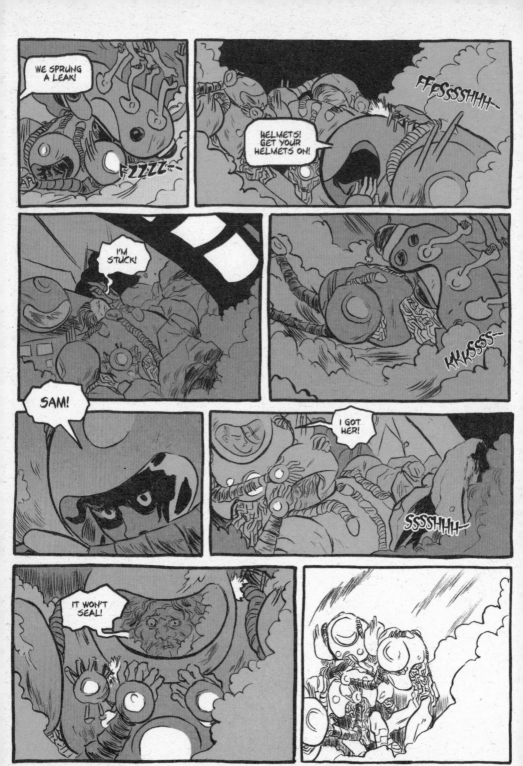

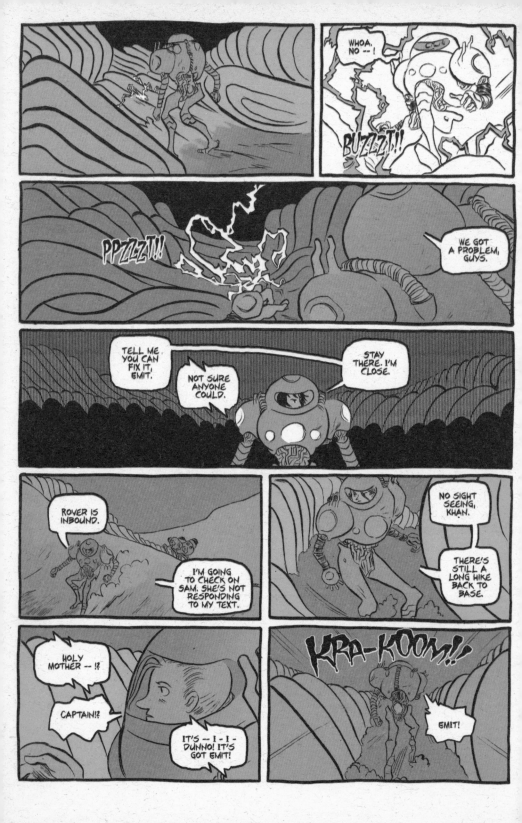

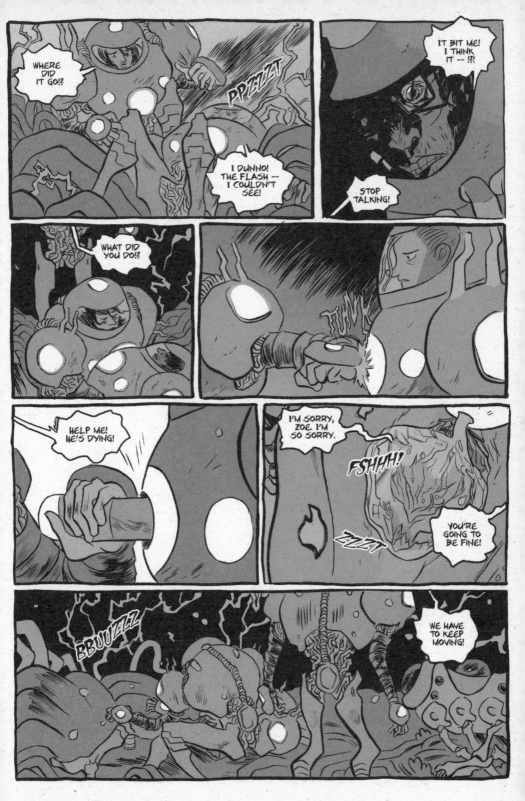

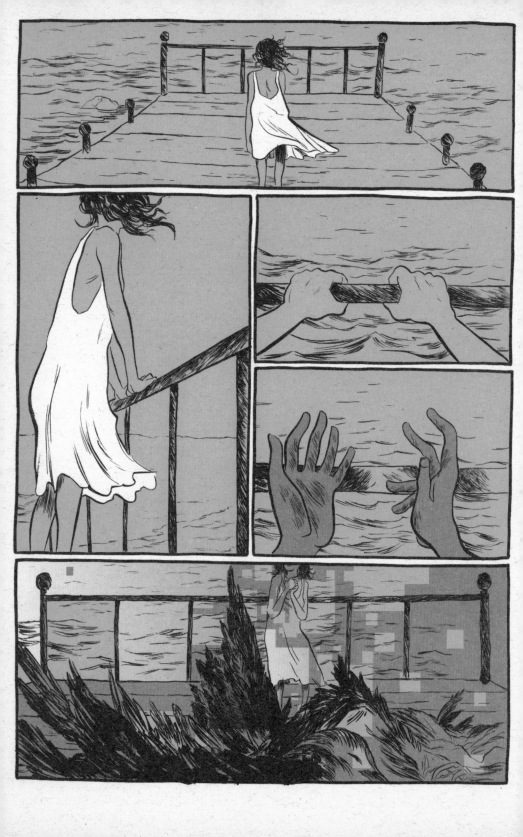

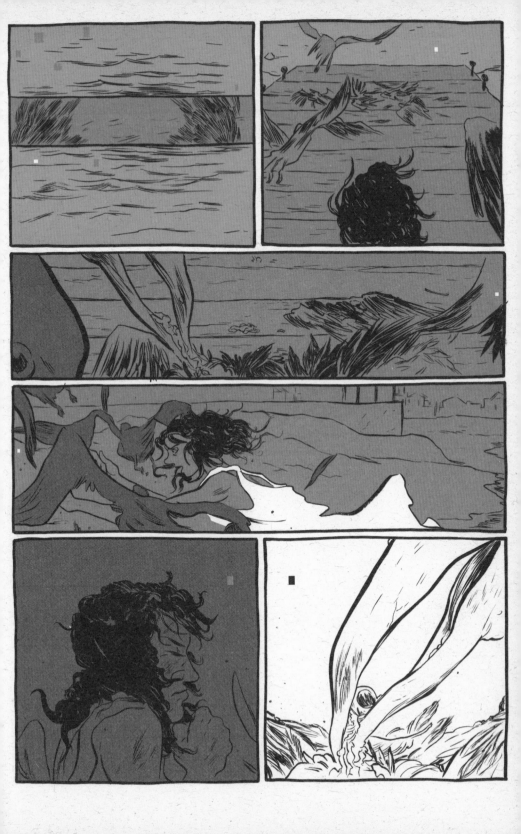

THERE WAS A SURGE. THE COILS OVER-LOADED. YOU WERE HIT.

I DON'T REMEMBER --

THE CHAIN REACTION DESTROYED OUR ONLY POWER SOURCE. WE'VE ONLY GOT 20 HOURS LEFT ON THE BATTERIES.

JUST LONG ENOUGH TO MAKE IT THROUGH THE NIGHT.

EMIT!?

HE LOST A LOT OF BLOOD.

DIDN'T SURVIVE THE TRIP BACK.

I SAW SOMETHING. IT ATTACKED US.

YOU'RE IN SHOCK.

LISTEN TO ME. NONE OF THIS WAS AN ACCIDENT.

TAKE YOUR HANDS OFF ME!

IT'S HUNTING US!

I'M RELIEVING YOU OF COMMAND.

YOU CAN'T --!

NURSE!

TOK!

OOF!

DON'T MAKE THIS HARDER THAN IT HAS TO BE.

I WILL FIGHT YOU TO MY LAST BREATH.

THEN WE DO THIS BY THE BOOK.

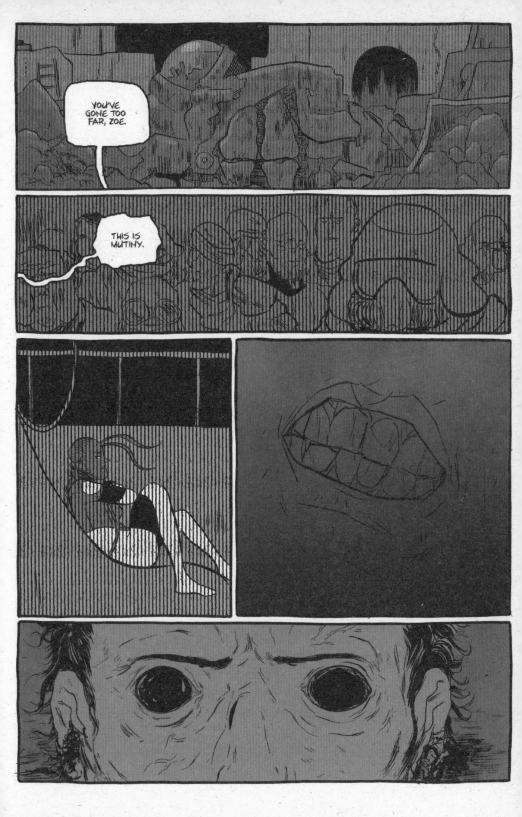

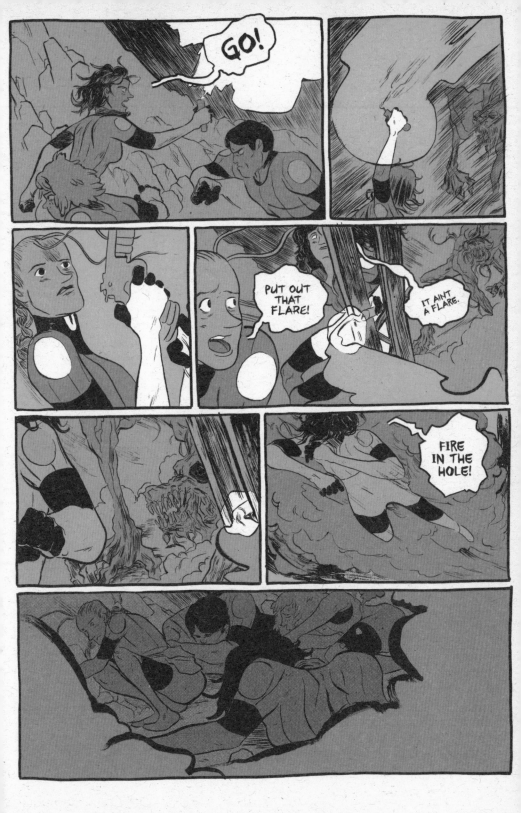

TWO AT A TIME.

HURRY!

I'M AFRAID OF HEIGHTS.

TECHNICALLY WE'RE UNDERGROUND.

HOW THE HELL DID YOU BECOME AN ASTRONAUT, RAJ?

I WANTED TO BE A TEACHER BUT THERE'S A RECESSION...

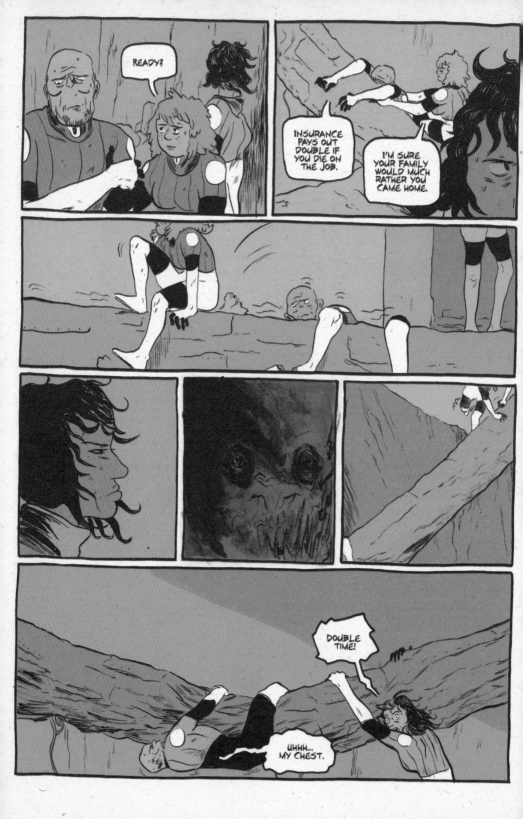

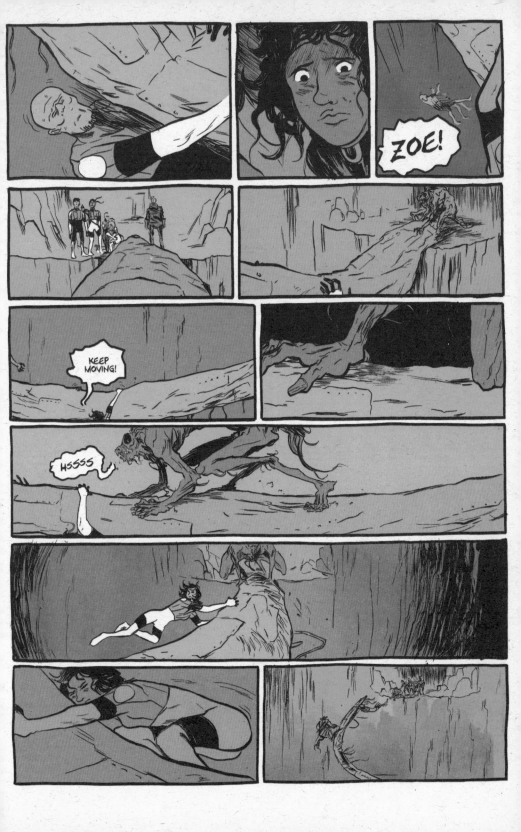

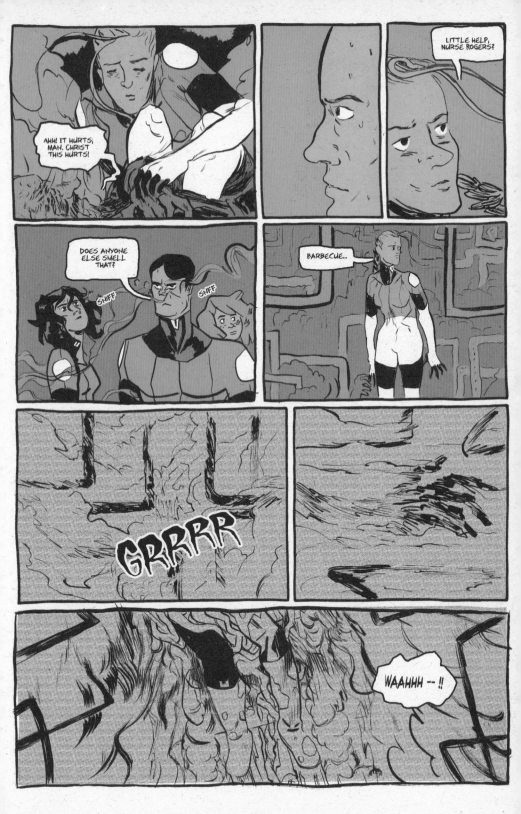

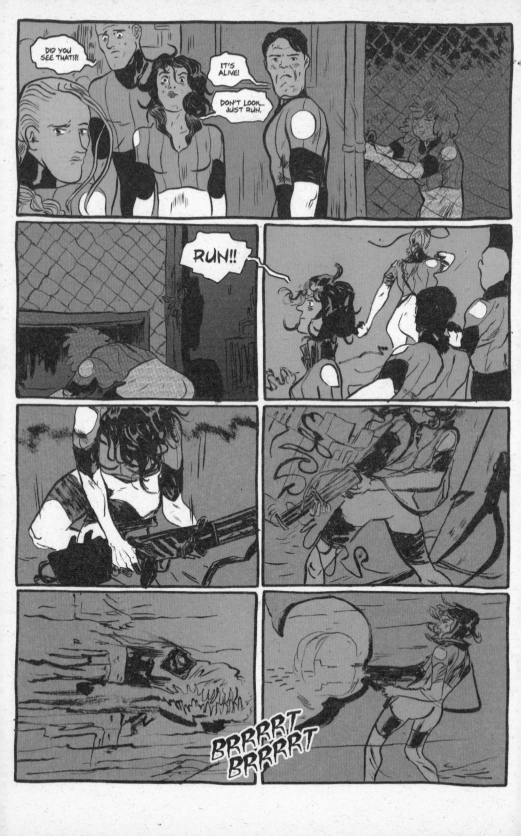

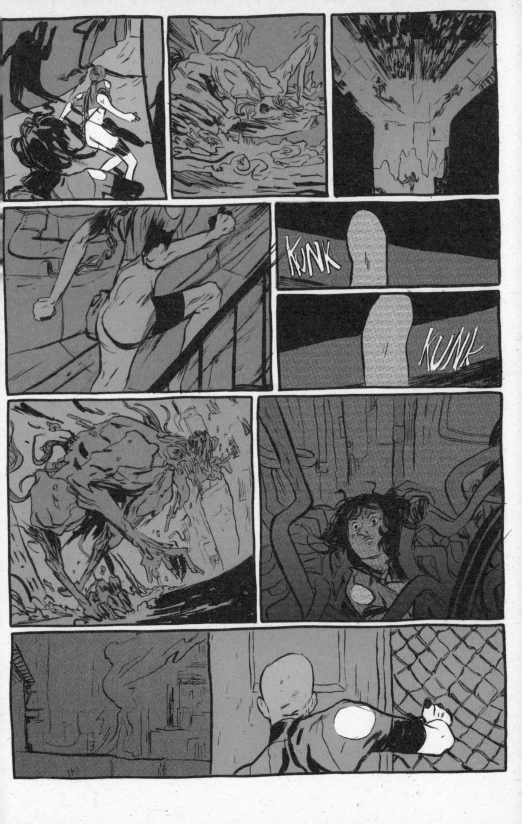

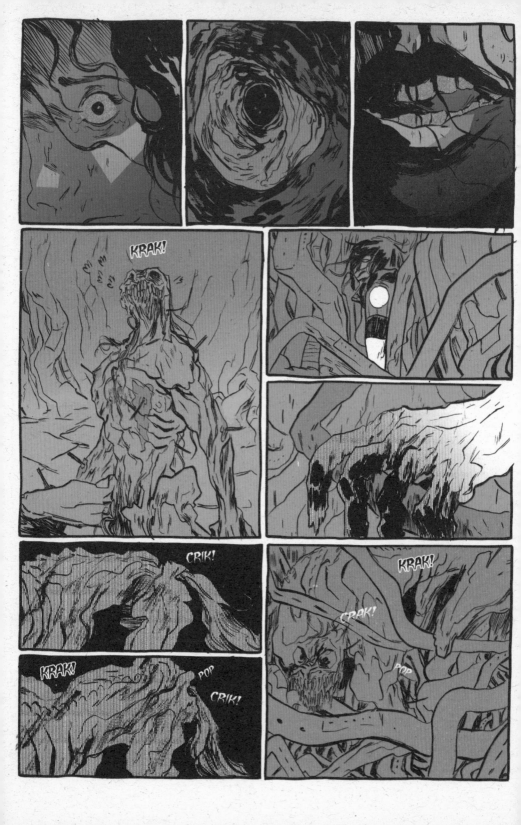

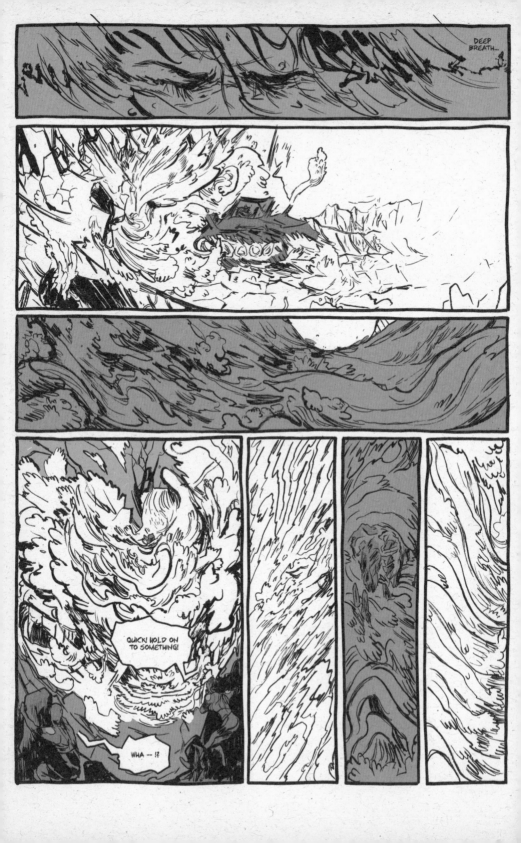

CORNY.

WHICH ONE IS KHAN'S?

WHY?

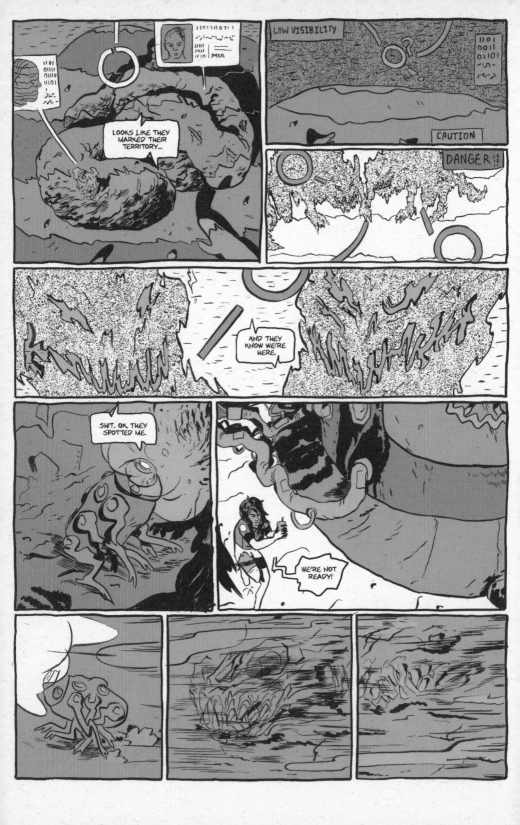

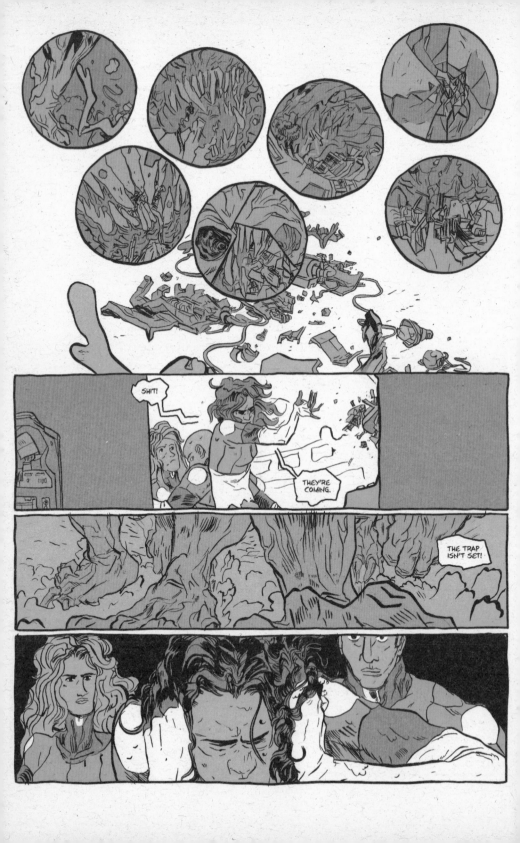

IT'S ALL ABOUT THE ANGLES.

SNIFF
SNIFF

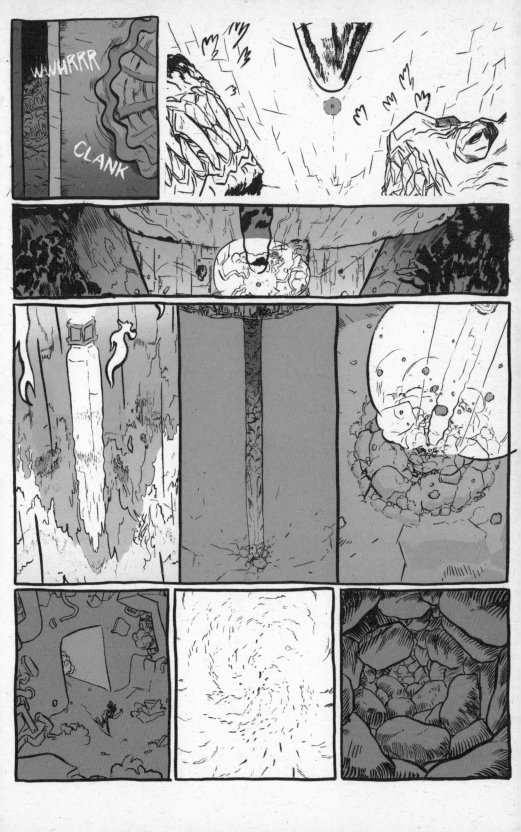

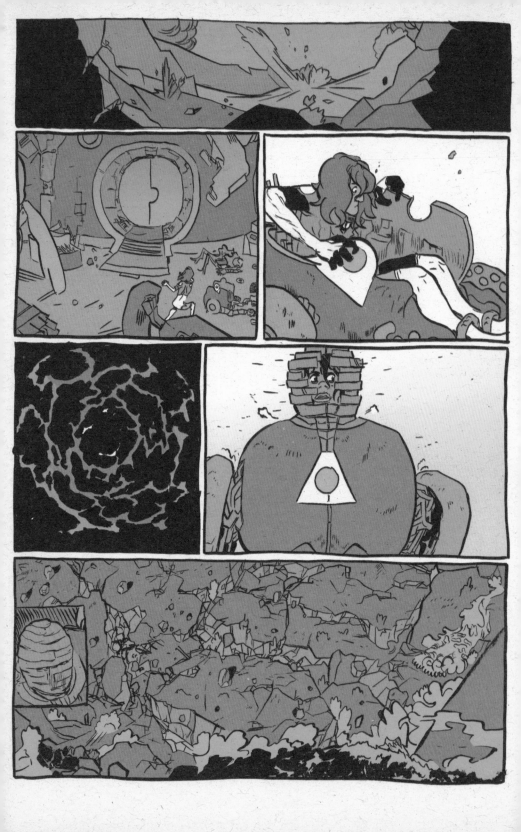

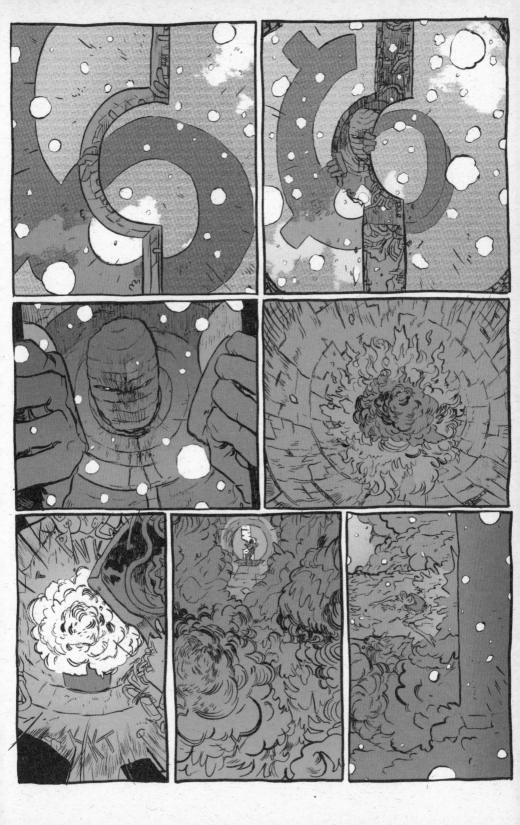

TONY TROV

is a writer/musician/soup enthusiast. He and Johnny Zito worked on BLACK CHERRY BOMBSHELLS, LA MORTE SISTERS, CARNIVALE DE ROBOTIQUE and MOON GIRL. If granted permission he will pet your dog. Follow him @TonyTrov

JOHNNY ZITO

is a writer/artist who lives in a big South Philly row home with his friends. They stay up late, playing laser tag and reading comic books. He and Tony Trov created South Fellini, their Intellectual property studio. They've created series for Comixology, Red 5 Comics, and High Treason Pictures. Follow him @JohnnyZito

CHRISTIAN WESIER

is a filmmaker/writer/producer, stuck in a state of the perpetual hustle. DOGS OF MARS is his first comic book, but he hopes for more. He currently resides in North Wildwood, New Jersey, and dreads moving back to Los Angeles.

PAUL MAYBURY

is an Award-winning artist and writer whose work has been featured by Marvel, DC, Dark Horse, Heavy Metal, Ubisoft, Metro, Image, Criterion and Fast Company. He lives in Houston, Texas. This work is dedicated to his parents, Paul and Silvia.

GABE BAUTISTA

is SENOR GABRIEL BAUTISTA JR. COMIX GORILLA. COLORIST SHOGUN. An Eisner award winning colorist on THE SPIRIT and ALLSTAR WESTERN, published by DC Comics. He is the creator of comic battling site ENTERVOID. COM He draws Charley < 3's Robots in the issues of ELEPHANTMEN, published by Image.

WITH THANKS

Ricky Valenzuela   Kody Chamberlain

Vitoria Elliott   Rahzzah

Jordan Gibson   Canson

Lon Dekkars   Erik Larsen

Loston Wallace   Sheldon Vella

Rob Guillory   Katy Riggs

EMIT   ISAIAH   KHAN   ZOE

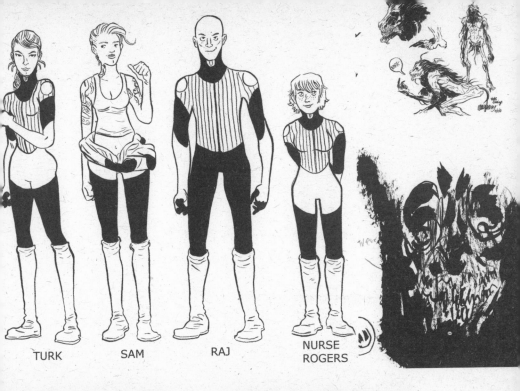

TURK   SAM   RAJ   NURSE
                     ROGERS

GUEST PIN-UPS

Steve Funnell
Viktor Kalvachev
Alexis Ziritt
Christine Larsen
Giannis Milonogiannis
Michel Fiffe
Rob Guillory
Jordan Gibson and Victoria Grace Elliot

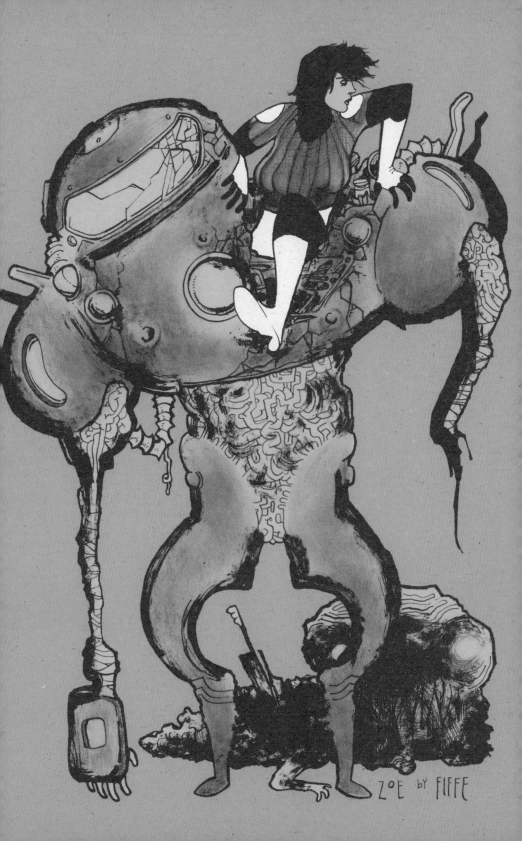

ZOE by FIFFE

Original four covers as they appeared on Comixology.

Art by Rahzzah